ORBIT

Sir Isaac Newton (Yerkes Observatory)

ORBIT:

A PICTURE STORY OF FORCE AND MOTION

BY HY RUCHLIS

Drawings by Alice Hirsh

HARPER & BROTHERS PUBLISHERS NEW YORK

This book is dedicated to
Carol, Michael, and all other young people
in the hope and belief
that they will never have reason to fear
man's conquest of outer space.

CONTENTS

ORBIT

INTRODUCTION

With the arrival of Sputnik, the first earth satellite, we began a new era of exploration far more exciting than any witnessed before.

Books of the future will give due credit to the Russians for being the first to take this step. But they will also record the fact that space flight was not the result of the work of any one man or any one country. It took the labors of thousands upon thousands of men from countries all over the globe to make space flight a reality. Englishmen, Italians, Frenchmen, Germans, and Americans participated in this immense task, as well as Russians. Space flight is the fruit of a gigantic international effort of scientists, engineers, inventors, and machinists who put their brains to work to solve the many problems that had to be overcome.

But if we want to select one particular person who may be said to have done the most to make space flight possible, Sir Isaac Newton stands out as the superpioneer. Way back in 1686 he developed theories to explain the way in which the moon and planets move in their orbits. He created the mathematics which space fliers must use to plan their flights. He showed how to calculate exactly how much speed an earth satellite would need to stay in an orbit, and how fast it would have to go to escape from the earth completely.

If Sir Isaac Newton could come back to life and walk into the room where the flight of a space ship is being planned, he would be amazed at the speed with which our modern computing machines work. They perform calculations in minutes that once required years of intense labor by dozens of mathematicians. But he would be very pleased to know that the formulas which he presented to the world in 1686 are the same ones fed into the computers to guide them in planning an earth satellite orbit or a space flight.

Why did Newton work out these laws and formulas? He needed them to explain why the moon revolved about the earth, and why the planets revolved about the sun. In the course of solving these problems he also solved, at least in theory, those of space flight and earth satellites. It required more than two and one-half centuries of scientific and engineering work to bring his ideas to reality.

Newton did more than set the pattern for computing orbits of planets and man-made satellites. He even indicated the kind of motor that would be needed for space flight. He drew no blueprints for the machinery, but he did specify in his Laws of Motion how *all* things move. From his analysis we are able to understand how we walk, how we jump, and how we row a boat. Using Newton's Laws of Motion we were able to work out the mechanism for making a car move and an airplane fly. From the information he gave us we know that only a rocket type of engine can take us out of the earth's atmosphere, and we can estimate how much power and fuel the engine needs.

Every engineer starts his career in college by plunging directly into a study of Newton's laws and of the mathematics he devised—the calculus. It does not matter whether he plans to study electronics, chemistry, the strength of bridges, or atoms. He will use Newton's laws and calculus throughout his life in solving the most practical of problems, as well as the most abstract.

Look about you at the results of Newton's work. Cars stream along highways. Ocean liners glide majestically across the sea. Trains rumble along the countryside, carrying goods and people to and fro. None of these vehicles could have been perfected if Newton had not worked out his theories.

Without Newton's work our modern industrial civilization could not have developed.

In the pages that follow you will read about Newton's laws and see how they are exemplified in everyday life as well as in earth satellites. You will see how the same forces that govern walking also control the flight of space ships.

Since all of us like to know where we are going, we shall here draw the main outlines of Newton's Laws of Motion before we proceed to go into them in detail.

Newton set up three Laws of Motion.

The first law deals with *inertia*—the tendency of

objects to maintain whatever motion they have without change.

The second law deals with *acceleration* and *momentum*—the way in which objects speed up or slow down.

The third law deals with *action and reaction*—the way in which any action an object takes always results in an equal and opposite reaction.

In addition to these three Laws of Motion Newton worked out his Law of Gravitation, which enabled him to calculate the gravity force that any object in the universe has upon any other. With this theoretical basis he was then able to solve the problems of orbits of planets and moons.

The job that he did was so good that scientists can pinpoint the position of any planet or moon, with an amazing degree of accuracy, centuries into the future. In fact, when they find any of their predictions to be wrong, they first suspect the presence of unknown planets or forces that are causing the observed differences. That is how the planets Neptune and Pluto were discovered. You will read more about this absorbing story later in the book.

It may seem inappropriate to start this book with a chicken dinner on a table, but that's exactly what we are going to do. You will find that a chicken dinner can reveal important clues to enable us to understand earth satellite orbits.

1. INERTIA

FIG. 1 shows a chicken dinner suspended in midair. Offhand, you might think that the picture was the result of a photographic trick. But that isn't true. A brief moment before the picture was taken, the chicken dinner had been sitting on a table, as all good chicken dinners should.

However, the table in this case is not an ordinary one. It is a special high-speed sled used in testing airplane equipment. The picture was snapped by a high-speed camera just after the table had catapulted out from under the dinner.

The "table" may be seen at the right side of the photo disappearing from under the dishes. It moved so rapidly that it left the dinner behind, in midair, just beginning to fall. A fraction of a second after this high-speed photo was taken the dinner completed its fall and hit the mechanism below.

This picture illustrates one part of Newton's Law of Inertia. *An object at rest tends to remain at rest.* The chicken dinner tended to remain where it was when the sled was catapulted forward.

Fig. 1. Chicken dinner in midair. (Northrup Aircraft, Inc.)

A good magician can perform the same stunt by pulling a cloth from under the dishes on a table. If he pulls the cloth rapidly enough, the dishes will be left standing as they were.

The unhappy driver whose truck is shown rearing up on its "hind legs" in Fig. 2 would do well to learn the lesson given to us by the chicken dinner of Fig. 1.

You have noticed when standing in a bus that you tend to fall backward toward the rear as the bus starts up. According to the Law of Inertia, you tend to remain where you are when the bus starts moving. The bus therefore pulls out from under you. But since your feet are touching the floor of the bus, they tend to be pulled along. Only if you brace yourself

Fig. 2. A rearing truck. (International News Photo)

or hold onto something in the bus can you avoid a fall when it starts up rapidly.

Try pushing a car. It has such a great tendency to remain at rest that a very large force is needed to budge it. It has a great deal of inertia of rest.

Now let's get back to the truck in the photo. It had come to a stop. Then the driver stepped on the gas to start moving forward again. The load of wood in back tended to remain where it was. The truck body pulled out from under the wood. The load then shifted to the back. Now it overbalanced the weight of the front part of the truck. Like a seesaw, the front end went up and the back went down.

To get the truck back to its normal position the driver will have to unload its cargo until the front end overbalances the back end and the front wheels come down. Then he will have to rearrange his cargo so that the rear of his truck doesn't go down again the next time he steps on the gas.

If the driver had known more about science, he might have prevented this mishap by reducing his load, fastening it with rope, or by starting up more gradually.

Inertia can cause trouble in vehicles not only when they are starting up but also when they are slowing down and turning. As we shall soon see, inertia of rest is only one part of the story.

INERTIA OF MOVING OBJECTS

The car shown in Fig. 3 seems about to take off

Fig. 3. Inertia makes this car fly. *(Ford Motor Co.)*

into the wild blue yonder. But you know that its flight will only be temporary. Gravity will soon take over and bring it back to earth.

We have already described that part of Newton's Law of Inertia which deals with objects at rest. Now we complete the law by adding another part dealing with moving objects. *An object in motion tends to remain in motion with the same speed and in the same direction.*

The car in Fig. 3 had just climbed the hill at top speed. When the road suddenly curved downward at the top of the hill, the car tended to keep going in a straight line at the same speed. So it shot up into the air, away from the road. Of course, this can only

9

happen if the speed is great enough. At slow speeds there is enough time for gravity to act to keep the car safely on the road.

Like our flying auto, the roller coaster of Fig. 4 tends to fly straight off into space at the top of the ride. But it doesn't go quite fast enough to do so. However, the people in the roller coaster have insides that can move around to some extent. And they feel the effects of inertia inside their bodies as they zoom around the track.

At the top of the incline a person's insides tend to keep going straight ahead into space and therefore press upward against the body wall. At the bottom of the incline one's insides tend to keep going downward and so press downward against the body wall. Around a curve to the left the insides tend to move straight ahead and so press against the right side of the body. The opposite happens on a curve to the right.

THE EARTH'S MOTION

In olden times people believed that the earth stood still and that the sun revolved around it. One of the main arguments against a moving earth was that no motion was felt. But we know that the earth is moving at a speed of about 18 miles a second as it travels around the sun. Shouldn't we feel this enormous motion?

Fig. 5 provides an important clue to this puzzle. A coin and a cigarette are shown balanced upright

Fig. 4. Inertia causes that funny feeling in the pit of your stomach. *(Steeple-chase Park, Coney Island)*

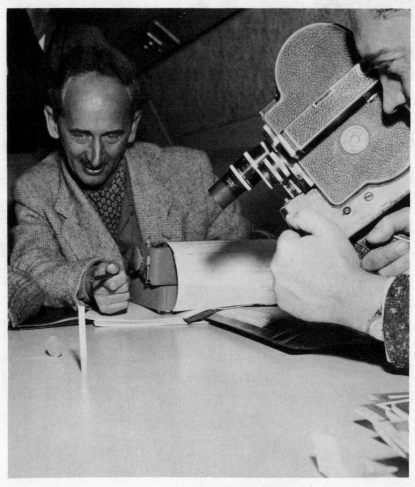

Fig. 5. This coin and cigarette balance on edge even though moving in an airplane at 692 miles per hour. *(Boeing Airplane Co.)*

on a table. There seems to be nothing very unusual about that. But this picture was taken in an airplane flying at a speed of 692 miles an hour! And this great speed had no effect on the coin and cigarette. Why?

According to the Law of Inertia the coin and cigarette traveling at 692 miles an hour in the airplane will tend to keep going at that speed in the same direction. All the pilot has to do to keep them from toppling over is to maintain a steady speed in level flight—no matter whether that speed is 692 miles an hour or 60 miles an hour. At a steady speed, no matter how great, coins, people, instruments, and any other objects in the airplane will keep going at that speed. If the airplane were vibrationless, noiseless, and completely closed off from a view of the outside, it would be impossible to detect the fact that the plane is in rapid motion.

But as soon as the airplane departs in any way from that steady straight-line motion, that fact would immediately be noticed in some way. The coin and cigarette would fall over. People would feel their insides moving around. They would feel their bodies being pushed to one side of the airplane or the other.

We usually feel the motions of vehicles, even at steady speeds, because of vibrations caused by the motion. In that case we feel the slight motions under us as the vehicle shakes around while we travel straight onward. If the vibrations are reduced sufficiently, we no longer feel any motion at all at steady speed in the same direction. In fact, that's the point of Fig. 5. The manufacturer of the airplane took this picture to show that vibrations have been reduced to the point where even a coin can be made to balance on edge.

You can now see why people do not feel the motion of the earth. Our globe travels in practically a straight line at steady speed without vibrations. Our inertia keeps us going at the same speed as the earth, and therefore it seems to us to be standing still.

We said the earth travels in "practically" a straight line because that line really isn't exactly straight. The earth turns around once a day as it moves through space. But this rotation is so gradual that our straight-line motion changes extremely slowly throughout the day, and we never notice it. The change in the earth's straight-line motion due to its once-a-year revolution around the sun is even more gradual, and therefore even harder to detect. Thus for practical purposes we may consider our motion through space as practically in a straight line at any given moment.

2. FORCE AND INERTIA

IN Fig. 6 we clearly see the straight-line motion of the rockets that have just left the airplane. But we also notice something new. If inertia alone were acting, we would expect to see the rockets alongside the airplane, not ahead of it.

Each rocket has its own "motor," exerting force to push it forward. As a result of this forward push, inertia is overcome and the rocket is made to speed up and pull ahead of the airplane.

Force can overcome inertia. It can change motion. In the case of the rockets shown in Fig. 6 the force causes an acceleration (speeding up) because it is pushing from behind the rocket. If the force acted at the front, pushing backward, then it would cause a *deceleration* (slowing down).

Fig. 6. The rockets pick up speed because a force is used to overcome inertia. (Republic Aircraft Co.)

Inertia can create enormous forces. Fig. 7 shows Colonel John P. Stapp during a record-breaking land run of 421 miles per hour. The vehicle in which this was accomplished is a specially designed rocket-propelled sled, riding on tracks. The track is only about two-thirds of a mile long. Yet in that short distance the sled was speeded up to 421 miles an hour, and then braked to a stop as scoops underneath the sled plowed into a trough of water.

During the acceleration and deceleration of this run Colonel Stapp was subjected to inertia forces more than 40 times those created in a car when the brakes are jammed on at high speed.

Fig. 7A shows him pressed back against his seat as six rockets force the sled forward, faster and faster. Inertia, the tendency to remain where he was at the start, presses him tightly against the back of his seat. At the same time the air in front of him has inertia and resists being pushed out of the way by his body. Notice the facial distortions that result from this *air resistance*.

Fig. 7B shows what happens when the sled's scoops

Fig. 7. When this sled, traveling at 421 miles an hour, is braked to a short stop, enormous forces are created because of inertia. *(Northrup Aircraft, Inc.)*

A

B

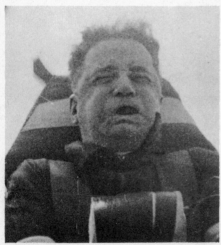

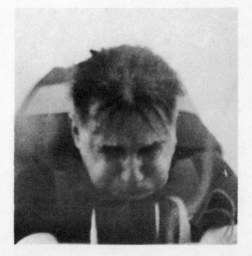

hit the water in a trough under the track after the rockets have stopped pushing. The inertia of rest of the water creates a resistance which rapidly slows down the sled. During this deceleration, Colonel Stapp's tendency to keep going at 421 miles per hour hurls him forward. Notice how his head is supported in front by a pad, while heavy straps prevent his body from flying forward.

Some of the men partaking in these tests have been subjected to forces as high as 45g. This means that a person undergoing such a force experiences the equivalent of 45 times his normal weight. Such large forces can only be withstood for very short periods of time.

You may wonder why such experiments are performed at all. Why do men subject themselves to this type of torture?

The experiment shown in Fig. 7 was designed to help develop equipment to permit a jet flier to parachute out of a high-speed airplane. The designers of such equipment must know how strong to make the straps that hold the flier in place. They want to find out what kind of support is needed for different parts of the body in order for the flier to survive the enormous forces that result from sudden changes in speed.

These experiments will also aid in the design of space ships. A space ship blasting off from the earth must pick up enormous speed in a very short time. A speed of 25,000 miles per hour might have to be reached in three minutes. The inertia of rest of the

17

passengers in such a ship would cause them to be hurled downward with a force of about 6g. Every piece of equipment in the ship must be securely fastened and constructed to withstand such a force. The passengers will need special supports in order to remain alive. Thus, the kind of experiment performed by Colonel Stapp is necessary to prepare for space flight as well as for jet flight.

INERTIA AND ACCIDENTS

Inertia is the main cause of injury and damage during auto accidents. The truck in Fig. 8 had attempted to make a turn on an icy road. Inertia made it tend to keep going in a straight line. With its tires

Fig. 8. Inertia is the basic cause of most accidents. (Wide World Photo)

unable to grip the road to force it into the turn, the truck skidded and crashed into the store. Its tendency to keep going made it push in the front of the store. And the tendency of the store to remain where it was pushed back at the truck and damaged it.

In every crash there are always these two inertia tendencies at work. The moving vehicle has inertia of motion and tends to keep going. The object that is struck has inertia of rest and tends to remain still. Both are therefore damaged, as enormous forces are created by inertia.

The greater the speed, the greater the inertia of the moving object, the harder it is to stop, and the greater the damage when it hits something. That is why high speed on the road is so dangerous.

Inertia can play gruesome tricks during auto accidents. For example, we see in Fig. 9 how a cigarette that had been in a passenger's mouth was pushed right through the glass windshield of a car during a head-on collision. At high speeds, even very light objects can exert tremendous forces because of their tendency to keep moving.

Forces resulting from inertia cause very peculiar effects. Straws, driven at great speeds, have been known to pierce planks of wood during hurricanes. Wooden planks have passed right through the trunks of trees. A bullet, a harmless piece of metal when outside the gun, can kill and destroy because of its inertia at high speed. A meteorite traveling at about ten miles a second could destroy a space ship by puncturing its walls as easily as we crack an egg-

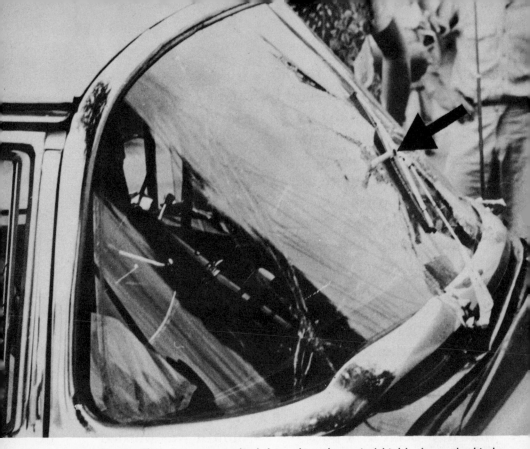

Fig. 9. This cigarette, pushed through a glass windshield, shows the kind of nasty trick that inertia can play during a crash. *(United Press Photo)*

shell. Vital instruments and the rocket engine could be put out of commission by such a "bullet."

Many people know nothing about inertia and have no respect for its power. Walk down the street and take a look at the back shelves of the cars parked along the curb. You will see all sorts of objects from metal toys to traveling irons. Each of these could kill a passenger if the car made a sudden stop or crashed. The inertia of such objects could make them fly forward at high speed if the car stopped suddenly.

You will frequently see an unthinking parent permitting his precious child to walk around on the front seat without any protection whatsoever. During a sudden stop, inertia could hurl the child forward to serious injury, or worse.

The lesson is clear. Have respect for inertia.

AN INERTIA PROBLEM

At this point you have learned enough about inertia to try your hand at solving a problem.

Fig. 10 shows a car that has just rammed a hydrant and broken off its top. The rear of the car has been lifted high into the air by the gushing water. Can you think of four ways in which inertia played a part in this curious accident? After you have figured out your answer, turn to page 142 and compare the answer with yours.

Fig. 10. Can you find four ways in which inertia was responsible for this strange accident? (Wide World Photo)

3. THE FORCE OF FRICTION

INERTIA seems a simple idea. Yet it took mankind a long time to realize its full meaning, as expressed by Newton. The trouble is that inertia is usually disguised. The force of friction gets in the way and masks inertia effects.

For example, a sled is much harder to move on sand than on ice. This seems to show that the sled has a different amount of inertia of rest. On the other hand, even if you push a sled on ice on level ground and then let it coast, it slows down and stops. If you try the same thing on a cement sidewalk, the sled will slow down much sooner or barely move at all. This would appear to show that moving things have a tendency to slow down, rather than to keep going.

The difficulty is that the sled is rubbing against the cement, or against the ice. The slight roughnesses in the two rubbing objects grip each other and tend to prevent motion.

In Fig. 11 you see a simple kind of friction test. Similar objects are placed on a slanted board on different kinds of material and the board is tilted until they slide down. The board on the right, which is still gripping its object, has the most friction. In this case the material is specially designed rubber for conveyor belts. A great deal of friction is an advantage for such a purpose.

The test in Fig. 11 shows that the amount of friction differs for various surfaces in contact with each other. As a result the effects of inertia are disguised so that we frequently cannot recognize them. For example, in Fig. 1 (the chicken dinner in midair) what would have happened if the sled had been pulled slowly instead of being catapulted? The dishes would have gone along with the sled. Some would have toppled over. But the tendency to remain at rest would have been hidden. Only with a rapid catapulting action could the force of friction be overcome sufficiently so that we could see the inertia effect clearly.

Fig. 11. This simple test measures the amount of friction between two surfaces. (United States Rubber Co.)

Although Newton did not have any frictionless laboratory to help him in discovering the Law of Inertia, he did have a giant astronomical "laboratory" to gather his facts. Out in space, planets and satellites do not rub against each other. There is no friction between a moving planet and the space through which it moves. With the confusion caused by friction eliminated, Newton was able to express his laws insofar as they applied to the planets. Then the role of friction on earth was seen more clearly and everyday motions could be explained.

We must hasten to modify our statements about the lack of friction out in space. Perhaps we should say that there is *practically* no friction. Extremely small friction forces have been detected which operate through the centuries to change the motions of the moon and planets. For example, the moon causes the tides on earth, as we shall see later in the book. The relatively slight friction effects of the tides cause the speed of rotation of the earth to be reduced. Consequently the day becomes longer by a fraction of a second every century.

You have read of the fact that an earth satellite must be hurled up to a very high altitude before it is possible for it to follow an orbit around the earth. At the five-mile-a-second speed required by an earth satellite, friction with air at lower levels would be great enough to heat it to melting temperature and cause it to disintegrate.

And even if the earth satellite could be made to

withstand such temperatures, friction of the air would slow it down to a point where it would no longer follow a permanent orbit. The satellite would simply fall back to earth. Thus an earth satellite can keep revolving about the earth only at heights of several hundred miles, where there is almost no air.

FRICTION IN DAILY LIFE

Friction is a very important force in everyday life. Without it you could not walk or run. It enables you to grip the ground so as to push it. For that reason the soles of your shoes are made of high-friction material. You have trouble walking on ice because there is little friction. Your shoes do not hold against the ice and you are unable to push the ground to walk.

Cars and trains need friction to prevent the wheels from slipping. Nails and screws hold in wood, and sandpaper grinds down a surface, because of friction. Special friction materials are used in brakes so as to permit a driver to stop his car.

Much as we need friction in some cases, we find it a real nuisance in others. Consider the case of an automobile traveling along the road at 50 miles an hour. According to the law of inertia, the car tends to keep going at that speed. It would therefore seem that all one need do to maintain that speed is to shut off the motor and let the car coast. But friction spoils the picture by opposing the motion. If we just let the car coast, friction would soon cause it to slow down and finally stop. So, to keep the car going at a steady speed, we must overcome the force of friction by exerting a forward force. This situation is pictured in Fig. 12. At a steady speed the forces acting on a car are in balance. The forward push exerted by the motor and wheels is just enough to balance the backward force of friction.

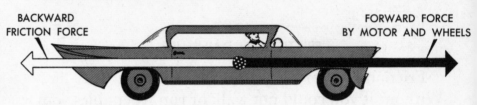

BACKWARD
FRICTION FORCE

FORWARD FORCE
BY MOTOR AND WHEELS

Fig. 12. When an automobile is moving at steady speed, the forces acting on it are balanced.

Suppose that while traveling at a steady speed we press a bit harder on the gas pedal. Now the forward force is greater than the backward force of friction. The forces are no longer balanced. The excess of forward force overcomes inertia and makes the car speed up. But friction soon catches up. As engine speed increases, the friction of moving parts inside the engine increases. Friction of the tires against the ground and air resistance become greater. Soon friction has caught up with the forward force of the engine. The two forces are once again balanced and the car no longer speeds up. It now moves along at a new steady speed—but faster than before.

We see that all of the force of the engine at steady speed goes to overcome friction. The billions of dollars we spend on gasoline to keep our cars and trucks rolling along the highways may therefore be blamed directly on the retarding effect of friction.

26

REDUCING FRICTION

Airplanes can travel at higher speeds than cars or boats because friction in the air is less than on the ground or on water. But at higher and higher speeds friction in the air increases so much that finally an airplane can go no faster with that particular engine.

Of course, a more powerful engine would make the airplane go faster. But then a new top speed is reached. In fact, at very high speeds the heat caused by the rubbing of the airplane against the air tends to heat up the metal and even to melt it. The main reason for the streamlined shape of fast airplanes is to reduce friction and thereby increase top speed (Fig. 13).

Fig. 13. Airplanes are streamlined to increase top speed by reducing friction. (Grumman Aircraft Engineering Corp.)

The wheel is usually considered to be the most important mechanical invention of all time. The rolling of wheels eliminates most of the friction caused by rubbing against the ground, and thus permits us to operate wagons, cars, trains, and trucks. With such a rolling vehicle we can transport many times as much cargo as can be moved by carrying it or dragging it along the ground.

Fig. 14 shows how rollers are used in a coal mine to help reduce friction and move heavy objects on a conveyor belt. The roller is simply a wide form of wheel.

Another method of reducing friction is to use a lubricant. Oil in engines separates the moving parts and thus reduces rubbing and friction. Water acts as a lubricant in ice skating, since the pressure on the blade caused by the weight of the skater melts the ice.

The degree of smoothness of a surface affects friction. Rough surfaces create large friction forces. If we make the surface smooth, there is a substantial reduction in friction force. Thus, a smoother paint on the outside of an airplane can actually enable it to reach a higher top speed.

A FRICTION PROBLEM

Now try your hand at a problem dealing with friction. In Fig. 15 we see two barges being tied together. (1) Why does the man in the photo wear gloves? (2) How does friction hold the barges to-

Fig. 14. Rollers are often used with conveyor belts to reduce friction and move cargo efficiently. *(United States Steel Corp.)*

gether? (3) Why do the coal piles all have the same slope?

Compare your answers with those on page 142.

Fig. 15. The action of friction is revealed in the way the coiled rope ties the barges together, in the use of gloves, and in the similar shape of the piles of coal. *(United States Steel Corp.)*

4. GRAVITY ON EARTH

FROM the day we are born to the day we die, the force of gravity controls our physical being. It takes a year or more after birth just to learn to stand up and walk. Every night we lie down to get a rest from gravity's constant pull.

Moving around is a problem mainly because of gravity. If gravity did not exist, we could move a giant ship around the world, using nothing more than a small rocket motor to lift it off the ground and get it started. With the extremely small amount of air friction at low speeds, we could move an enormous ship with an extremely small motor.

Space flight would be very easy if gravity could be eliminated or reduced greatly. A tiny rocket motor could easily take us to the moon.

GRAVITY IN EVERYDAY LIFE

But lest we think that gravity is just an unnecessary handicap to us, let us stop to consider that without it there would be no air to breathe, no water to drink, and no land to walk on. In fact, there would be no earth if it weren't for the force of gravity that keeps the land, oceans, and air pressing downward

31

toward its center. Without gravity, inertia would cause everything to fly off into space as the earth rotates.

Study Fig. 16 for a few minutes. Can you find 11 ways in which the effects of the force of gravity are revealed in this picture of Niagara Falls? Compare your answers with those on page 143. You may miss some of these effects simply because you are so accustomed to gravity as a basic part of your life.

Fig. 16 also indicates one way in which gravity is put to use by us. Most of Niagara's water is led by pipes to a powerhouse where the falling water turns giant turbines and generates electric power. Today about half our electricity is generated by using gravity force in this way.

Fig. 16. Can you find eleven ways in which gravity affects the objects in this picture? (Canadian Government Travel Bureau)

UP AND DOWN

Newton obtained an important clue in his analysis of gravity by taking inertia into account. The fact that all apples hang downward from tree branches shows that some force is pulling them toward the earth. Each apple has inertia of rest. To make it move and accelerate, a force is needed. We see the apple speed up (accelerate) when it falls. So we conclude that inertia is being overcome by some downward force. Newton called this force "gravity."

The earth is so large that we only see one small part of it and that little part seems flat to us. We might therefore think that people on the other side of the earth are standing "upside down." Actually, they are doing nothing of the kind. As you may see in Fig. 17, each person is pulled toward the center of the earth no matter where he is. So "down" is not one direction but many directions. "Down" in Europe is different from "down" in the United States. The only similarity between both "downs" is that they point straight toward the center of the earth.

HOW OBJECTS FALL

For thousands of years learned men believed that heavy objects fall faster than light ones because of their weight. They based this belief on the fact that light objects such as feathers fall very slowly in comparison with heavy objects. Their belief was backed up by the great prestige of the Greek philosopher Aristotle, whose word was almost law. So, when a

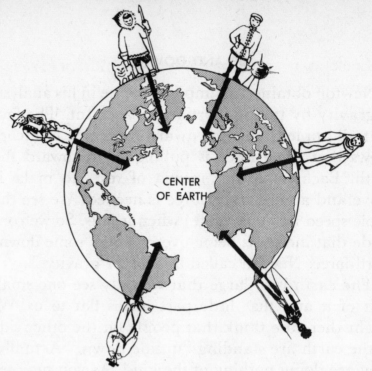

CENTER
OF EARTH

Fig. 17. Down is many directions on earth. It simply means "toward the center of the earth."

young upstart named Galileo tried to correct this belief in 1590, he ran into a great deal of opposition.

Of course a feather does fall more slowly than a rock. But the reason for this is not the feather's low weight but air resistance.

This can be shown by experiment in two ways. If we compare the rate of fall of a two-pound rock and a one-pound rock by dropping both from the same height at the same time, we find that they hit the ground together.

To clinch the point, we can drop a feather and a rock in a tube from which the air has been removed by a pump. The feather falls like the rock and hits the bottom at the same time.

Look at it this way. A two-pound rock weighs twice as much as a one-pound rock. That means it is pulled downward twice as hard by the force of gravity. So we imagine that it should fall faster.

But a two-pound rock also has twice as much inertia as a one-pound rock. Therefore it is twice as hard to move. As a result, twice as much pull on a rock that is twice as hard to move just balances out, and makes the two-pound rock move downward only as fast as the one-pound rock.

AIR RESISTANCE AND FALLING OBJECTS

If the force of gravity were the only thing acting on a falling object, we would expect it to fall faster and faster as it continues to be pulled downward by gravity. But as it speeds up it hits the air beneath it with greater and greater force. Inertia of the air causes it to resist being pushed out of the way. And the greater the speed of the falling object, the greater the resistance of the air being pushed aside. Finally, the air resistance is equal to the weight of the falling object and gravity force is then balanced. Now the object can no longer speed up. Inertia causes it to move downward at a steady speed.

Thus, most falling objects reach some steady speed after falling for a short time. For a man falling from an airplane this top speed is about 120 miles an hour. But if he is suspended from a parachute, his speed is reduced to a reasonably safe 12 miles an hour (Fig. 18).

Fig. 18. Air friction balances the force of gravity to give these parachutists a safe, steady rate of fall. (U. S. Air Force)

A parachute, by spreading out wide to catch a larger amount of air, increases air resistance. The weight of the man is then balanced at a much lower speed.

We find the same principle used in nature. The flying squirrel of Fig. 19 can leap from tree to tree safely, or even fall from a great height. He spreads out his legs and exposes wide folds of skin. These folds, together with a long bushy tail, act like a parachute to increase air resistance and slow him down to a safe falling speed.

Fig. 19. A flying squirrel makes use of air resistance to jump safely from great heights. (American Museum of Natural History)

5. INERTIA AND GRAVITY

THE car in Fig. 20 is using inertia to help it climb up a steep hill. It would have been unable to climb the hill from a standstill, since no car could remain on such a steep hill without being pulled down by gravity. But, by getting up high speed before the start of the climb, inertia, plus the push of the motor, enabled it to overcome the force of gravity and reach the top.

A similar thing happens when a ball is thrown up into the air. You give it as much inertia as possible by throwing it upward as hard as you can. Therefore, its inertia tends to make it keep going. But gravity acts to slow it down and finally makes it come to a momentary stop at the top of its rise. Now its inertia of rest is overcome and gravity pulls it downward faster and faster until it hits the ground.

It is interesting to note that the trip downward is exactly the reverse of the trip upward—if we disregard air friction. The ball slows down at a steady rate as it rises until the highest point is reached. Then on the way down it speeds up at exactly the same rate at which it slowed down on the way up. Finally it reaches the ground at about the same speed at which it left the earth. (Air friction reduces its speed somewhat.)

Fig. 20. Inertia helps overcome gravity to enable the car to reach the top of this very steep hill. *(Buick Motors)*

A LEAPING MOTORCYCLE

A falling object often has horizontal motion at the start of its fall. In that case the combination of inertia and gravity causes it to follow a curved path. For example, the motorcyclist in Fig. 21 can clear the men on the ground by taking advantage of inertia to offset the effect of gravity.

Newton showed that we can figure out the combined effects of inertia and gravity exactly as though each were acting independently. As an example, suppose that in a half-second the motorcycle in Fig. 22 falls four feet. Also suppose that in a half-second it travels forward 20 feet. Then from the moment it leaves the ramp we can predict the exact spot where it will be a half-second later, as shown in Fig. 22.

If only inertia were acting, the motorcycle would

Fig. 21. Inertia at high speed can carry this motorcycle safely past the men on the ground before gravity brings it back to earth. (*International News Photo*)

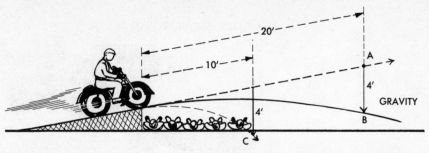

Fig. 22. Inertia and gravity act independently of each other to produce a parabolic path.

be at point A, 20 feet from the ramp, in a straight line with its top. Now draw a four-foot line straight down from point A. Gravity alone would make the motorcycle fall four feet from A. The two effects of inertia and gravity then combine to bring the motorcycle to point B, four feet below A.

If the motorcycle were going only half as fast, it would move forward only ten feet in a half-second instead of 20 feet. In that case the motorcycle would be at C instead of B a half-second after leaving the ramp. We see that the way to avoid hitting the men on the ground is simply to get up enough speed to clear them. Any speed greater than that will then always clear the men.

What's the purpose of the ramp? The incline gives the motorcycle inertia in a direction that slants upward at an angle. Thus it gets an upward motion. It will take some time for gravity's downward force to counteract this upward motion. By that time inertia has carried the motorcycle clear of the men on the ground.

We see a similar motion in Fig. 23. A car traveling at high speed leaps over another car and lands

Fig. 23. This car leaps into the air because of inertia and lands on

safely on another ramp. If the speed of the car and angle of the ramp are set in advance, the engineers who set up this experiment can predict how the car will hurtle through the air. A second ramp can then be set at the proper position and angle to permit a safe landing.

As in the case of the motorcycle in Fig. 21, inertia makes the car continue forward after leaving the ramp, while gravity gradually curves its path in a downward direction. Thus a similar type of path is followed.

PATH OF A PARACHUTIST

Fig. 24 shows a parachutist a short while after he jumped from the open door of a helicopter, and before his parachute was fully opened. Notice that he is directly below the open doorway of the helicopter. This would be easy to understand if the helicopter

42

the second ramp because of gravity. *(Chrysler Corp., Desoto Division)*

were hovering motionless. We would then say that gravity is pulling him straight down.

However, this is not quite the case. Notice how the parachute is being pushed backward by the motion of air. This means that the helicopter must be moving forward against the air. In that case, why should the parachutist be directly below the open door from which he has jumped?

This fact is explained when we remember that inertia and gravity act independently of each other. Suppose that the plane is moving forward at a speed of 30 feet a second. Then its passengers will also be traveling at that speed. When a person jumps out of the plane, he still keeps that forward speed. Therefore he will always be below the open door, unless pushed back by the air.

At the same time gravity acts independently to pull him downward from the level of the airplane. It

Fig. 24. The parachutist remains directly below the open door of the moving helicopter because inertia acts independently of gravity. (*Wide World Photo*)

has been found by experiment that if there is little air resistance any object falls 16 feet in one second, 64 feet in two seconds, and 144 feet in three seconds.

During one second the parachutist falls 16 feet. During the same second the ship moves forward 30 feet. Then the parachutist will be 16 feet below the airplane and 30 feet forward of the point from where he jumped, as shown at A in Fig. 25.

Fig. 25. How inertia and gravity combine to produce a parabolic path.

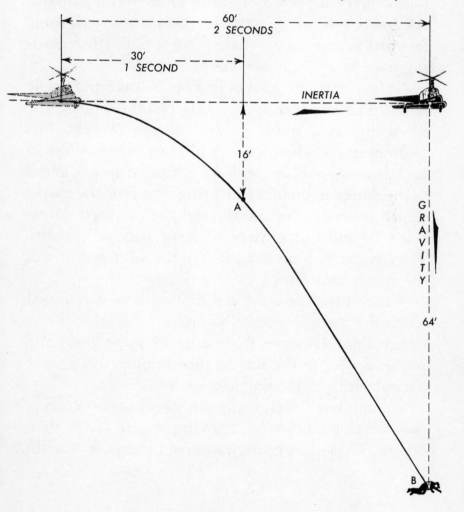

In two seconds the parachutist advances a total of 60 feet (2 × 30) because of inertia. In the same time he falls 64 feet. Thus after two seconds of fall he is at B, 64 feet down and 60 feet forward.

Where would he be after three seconds? Figure it out and then compare your answer with the one on page 144.

The paths of the motorcyclist in Fig. 21, of the flying car in Fig. 23, and of the parachutist in Fig. 24 follow a certain kind of curve known as a *parabola.* All freely falling objects which start out with some forward motion always take such a path (disregarding the effect of air resistance).

Notice how the sparks in Fig. 26 take parabolic paths. These sparks are glowing metal particles that shoot out as a result of the welding process. The photographer who took this picture kept the lens of his camera open for perhaps a second to get detail in the dark surroundings. During that time the sparks shot out because of inertia and then curved downward because of gravity to form parabolic paths. They registered their paths on the film because of the continuous glow.

Notice how the same parabolic shape is retained when the metal particles bounce off the table in the foreground. Observe that some of these bouncing particles veer to the side as they bounce, because of irregularities in the particles or in the table.

We can easily tell from the streaks that some of the metal particles are moving much faster than others. These fast particles move in almost straight

Fig. 26. Shooting sparks take parabolic paths. Can you tell which of these sparks are moving faster than others? (United States Steel Corp.)

paths. During the exposure time of the picture they moved forward much more than they fell. The slow ones have more sharply curved paths because they fell more than they moved forward.

The same kind of parabolic path is shown by the falling water shot from the hoses of the fireboat in Fig. 27. Each parabola is different because of the different positions of the hoses. The water may also be shooting out at different speeds.

Notice how the wind disrupts the parabolic shape. The wind is coming from the right. You can tell that by the way in which the streams are disrupted on the right side of the boat and seem to fall back. The wind also straightens out the paths of the streams on the left.

Fig. 27. Water from a hose takes a parabolic path, modified by the wind. (Black Star)

Fig. 28. Can you explain the parabolic path of these gasoline drums as they fall from the airplane? *(U. S. Air Force)*

DROPPING GASOLINE BARRELS

Now let's see how you can apply what you have learned to explain the very interesting formation of rubber gasoline barrels as they drop from a cargo airplane at a base in Greenland (Fig. 28). (1) Why are the barrels shot out the back, instead of being dropped straight down? (2) The formation seems to have a parabolic shape. How was it formed?

Figure it out if you can. Then turn to page 144 and compare the answer with yours.

6. TIDES AND GRAVITY

FIG. 29 shows a seashore scene with some strange rock pillars towering overhead. What would you think if we said that the peculiar shape of these rocks is due in part to the moon's gravity?

Far-fetched?

Not at all.

Most people think of gravity as the force that makes us fall down. But the moon overhead also exerts a force of gravity. It attracts us toward itself and tends to pull us upward! As a result we weigh a tiny fraction of an ounce less when the moon is overhead.

Don't think that this gravity force is too small to notice. The regular rise and fall of the tides are caused by the gravity force of the moon and, to a lesser amount, by that of the sun. The gravity force of the moon, aided by that of the sun, can pull the water of the oceans upward about six to eight feet to cause the tides.

Fig. 30 shows how the moon causes two water bulges on the earth, one on the near side and one on the far side. Why two bulges?

The moon attracts the water on the far side at A right through the earth, just as you are attracted to the earth right through the floor of your house. The moon attracts the main body of the earth at B a bit more strongly than the water at A because it is closer. The earth is thus pulled slightly away from the water at A, causing the bulge at A. The water at C is pulled more strongly by the moon than the earth at B because it is nearer. Therefore, the water bulges toward the moon at C. Thus, two tidal bulges are formed by the moon's gravity force.

As the earth rotates daily, these two bulges remain in a line with the moon. We may think of the earth as rotating under these bulges, thus causing the tides

Fig. 29. The gravity forces of the moon, sun, and earth, the earth's rotation, geography, and inertia of moving water combine to give these rocks their peculiar shape. *(New Brunswick Travel Bureau)*

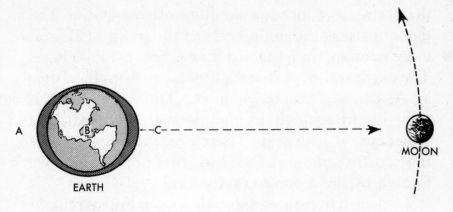

Fig. 30. The moon's gravity force is the main cause of the tides.

to rise and fall twice a day. Since the moon rises about 50 minutes later each day, the bulging of the water also occurs that much later.

Even though the sun is much bigger and heavier than the moon, its gravity effect on earth is less. This is so because the sun is about 400 times as far from the earth as is the moon. The moon therefore sets the timing of the tides, while the sun merely increases or decreases the amount of up-and-down movement.

Now, while tides are normally about six to eight feet in height, certain places on earth have higher tides because of geography. The peculiar rocks of Fig. 29 are located at Hopewell Cape on the Bay of Fundy on Canada's eastern shore, just north of Maine. This bay is shaped like a funnel. When the tidal water approaches the narrow end of the bay, it tends to pile up and cause tides as high as 50 feet!

As the waters of the high tide swirl around the crumbly sandstone of the cliffs at Hopewell, their

52

inertia of motion washes away some of the rock. Then the water drops about 25 feet at low tide to reveal the scene that you see in Fig. 29.

You can clearly see the point on the rocks reached by the high tides. In about six hours the distant water in Fig. 29 will rise and cover the shore up to the bulging parts of the rocks.

Eventually these rocks are undermined from below and the earth's gravity causes them to fall onto the shore. The cliff is thus eroded (worn away) by the combined effects of the moon's gravity, the sun's gravity, the earth's gravity, the earth's rotation, geography, and inertia of moving water.

7. THE LAW OF GRAVITATION

OUR everyday experience with the force of gravity makes it seem to us to be completely constant and unalterable. Actually, it is slightly different in various parts of the world. Fig. 31 shows a gravity meter in operation to detect underground oil. Oil is usually found under domes of rock. The changes in gravity force due to these rock domes give clues to their locations under the earth and therefore provide a way of locating oil.

CHANGING GRAVITY

As one climbs a mountain, gravity becomes slightly less because we are going away from the center of the earth. Gravity also gets slightly less as we move toward the equator. Thus a man who weighs 160 pounds in the United States would weigh about a half-pound less at the equator. If he went to the North Pole, his weight would increase by about a half-pound. The reasons for these gravity changes will be discussed later.

In Newton's time there was no equipment capable of measuring the earth's gravity or showing that it changed slightly on different parts of the earth. As

Fig. 31. This "gravity meter" helps detect underground oil by measuring slight differences in gravity force on the surface of the earth. (*Standard Oil Co. of N. J.*)

far as anyone could tell, a person's weight was the same anywhere.

But Newton wanted to find out what made the moon keep going around the earth. He therefore tried several theories. One of these assumed that gravity became less as one went away from the earth's surface. To solve his problem Newton had to guess how much less the force of gravity became at various distances from the earth. He finally found one solution that enabled him to explain the moon's revolution around the earth. He expressed this theory in what is today called the Law of Gravitation.

YOUR GRAVITY

According to this law, *all* objects in the universe attract each other with a force of gravity. The sun attracts the planets; the earth attracts the moon. The moon attracts the earth, the earth attracts you, you attract the earth—and you also attract nearby tables, chairs, and people.

You may wonder if this is really so. After all, nobody ever noticed *gravitational* attraction to other people or to objects or even to the earth. But, as we have seen, we do have instruments for measuring changes in the earth's gravity. And scientists have actually measured attractions between objects on earth. These gravitational attractions are very small. When you stand a foot away from another person, the force of attraction between you is only about 5/1,000,000,000 (five-billionths) of an ounce!

THE EARTH'S GRAVITY

Why do you feel the effects of the earth's gravity? Newton explained this by assuming that the force of gravity is greater for more massive objects. Think of the earth as being made of an enormous number of pieces of rock. Each rock pulls you with a slight force of gravity. But altogether, the slight pulls from trillions of trillions of rocks add up to a substantial force. Thus, gravity force increases with the mass of the objects pulling each other.

Why are you pulled toward the center of the earth? Some rocks underneath you, on your left, are pulling you down and somewhat to your left. But others under you, on your right, are pulling downward and to the right. Those underneath you are pulling straight down. All of these slight pulls average out to create one big pull straight down toward the center of the earth.

Why is the earth round? Suppose that the earth originally consisted of an irregular mass of loose rocks and other material. With every rock attracting every other rock, all of them had to come closer and closer until they touched. If there were high spots and low spots, the rocks on the higher places were pulled closer by moving into the lower places. This process stopped only when there were few high and low places of any significance on the earth and only when every part of the surface was about equally distant from the center. Thus a globe form was established for the earth by gravity.

You can see a somewhat similar process take place when a crowd forms on a beach. Suppose that some bathers are performing stunts. A crowd gathers. People can see better if they are nearer to the performers. Each person, attracted to the center, tries to get as close as he can, and will run around the outside, if necessary, to find a spot that is nearer. Thus, if an aerial photo were taken of the crowd on the beach, it would show a roughly circular form.

At this point you may wonder if the existence of high mountains doesn't contradict what we have just said. Shouldn't the mountains be pulled down? Try to imagine what the earth looks like from out in space. You will then see that the mountains are no more than tiny rough spots on the surface of the earth. In fact, if you could shrink the entire earth to the size of a billiard ball and hold it in your hand, it would appear to be quite smooth, like the billiard ball. Even a mountain such as Everest, more than five miles high, is extremely small compared with the 8,000-mile diameter of the earth. Even so, such mountains are constantly being worn down by gravity.

REDUCING GRAVITY

Now we come to that part of Newton's Law of Gravitation dealing with the way in which gravity is affected by distance. What happens to the force of gravity as an object goes away from the earth? Newton said that it becomes less, and he specified the exact amount of reduction.

Think of the earth as having a center somewhere under us. Since the diameter of the earth is 8,000 miles we may think of this center as being about 4,000 miles underground anywhere on the earth's surface. Now, with this center as the starting point for measuring distances, Newton stated that gravitational forces would change in the following way. At twice the distance from the center of the earth the force of gravity would become ½ × ½, or one-fourth as much. At three times the distance from the center of the earth, the gravity force would become ⅓ × ⅓, or one-ninth as much. What would it be four times as far from the center? You're right. It would be ¼ × ¼, or one-sixteenth as much.

Now let's imagine an enormous tower that goes up thousands of miles from the surface of the earth. Of course we can't build such a tower. But let's imagine one anyway.

After the tower is built, we send a 100-pound boy up to the top. At a distance of 4,000 miles from the ground he is 8,000 miles from the center of the earth (Fig. 32). Since he was 4,000 miles from the center

Fig. 32. Gravity force becomes less as we go away from the earth and finally disappears almost completely.

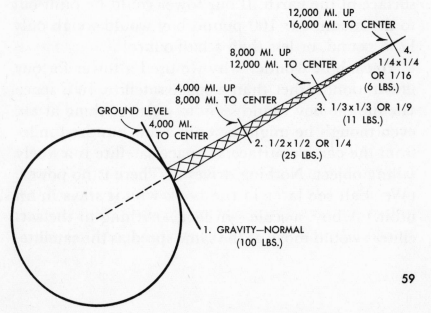

12,000 MI. UP
16,000 MI. TO CENTER

8,000 MI. UP
12,000 MI. TO CENTER

4. 1/4 x 1/4 OR 1/16
(6 LBS.)

4,000 MI. UP
8,000 MI. TO CENTER

3. 1/3 x 1/3 OR 1/9
(11 LBS.)

GROUND LEVEL
4,000 MI. TO CENTER

2. 1/2 x 1/2 OR 1/4
(25 LBS.)

1. GRAVITY—NORMAL
(100 LBS.)

of the earth when on the ground, he is now twice as far from the center. Gravity pulls him only ½ × ½ as strongly, and he therefore weighs one-fourth as much. His weight drops to 25 pounds from his original 100.

At a distance of 8,000 miles up, he is 12,000 miles from the center of the earth, and is now three times as far from the center as when he was on the ground. His weight is therefore ⅓ × ⅓, or one-ninth as much. He weighs one-ninth of 100 pounds, or about 11 pounds. At 12,000 miles up he is four times as far from the center of the earth and weighs ¼ × ¼, or one-sixteenth as much as on the surface of the earth. His weight would therefore be about six pounds.

At the moon's distance of about 240,000 miles from the earth, it is 60 times as far from the center of the earth as objects on the surface of the earth. The effect of gravity of the earth on the moon is therefore 1/60 × 1/60, or 1/3600 as much as on the surface of the earth. If our tower could be built out to the moon, our 100-pound boy would weigh only 1/36 pound, or less than a half ounce!

You might wonder why we used a tower for our illustration, rather than a space satellite. In a space satellite the boy would seem to weigh nothing at all, even though he might be only a few hundred miles from the earth's surface. A space satellite is a freely falling object. Nothing drives it. There is no power. (We shall see later in the book why it stays in an orbit.) A boy, a scale—in fact, anything in the satellite—would move at the same speed as the satellite.

Inertia and gravity would have a similar effect on all objects in the ship and they would all follow the same orbit. When the boy got on the scale it would fall away from him just as fast as he himself would fall toward earth. Thus there would be no push against the scale and it would read zero. Therefore we could not get a direct measurement of gravity on an earth satellite by using a scale.

You have read of the fact that animals in earth satellites experience a feeling of having no weight at all. If a person were placed in a closed capsule and dropped out of a rocket ship several hundred miles above the earth, he would start to fall toward the earth. But so would the capsule, and at an equal rate of speed. Thus as the person sped toward the floor, the floor would speed up by an equal amount in the same direction. The person in the capsule could never catch up to the floor unless he pulled or pushed himself toward it. In fact, a slight push could also send him "upward" inside the capsule and make his head hit the ceiling.

PROVING NEWTON'S LAWS

You may be wondering all this time how it is possible for us to be sure about things that might happen way out in space where no human being has as yet gone.

Suppose that you were an astronomer in charge of a big observatory. One day you get a letter from someone you don't know. The writer predicts the existence of a new planet, which nobody has as yet seen. Moreover, he tells you where to look for it in the sky. He predicts the way in which it will move. He tells you how heavy it is and estimates how bright it may appear.

Is he a crackpot? Should you throw the letter in the wastebasket or take up precious telescope time on a wild-goose chase?

If you were a scientist you wouldn't throw such a letter in the wastebasket too readily because you would know that Newton's Laws make such predictions possible.

For a long time before the discovery of Neptune in 1846, the existence of a planet farther from the sun than Uranus was suspected because of the fact that the observed orbit of Uranus did not quite agree with calculations for it. Either Newton's Laws, used in the calculations, were wrong or an unknown influence was at work.

In September, 1845, John C. Adams, a young English scientist, wrote to an astronomer suggesting that he look for a new planet in the sky—a planet whose existence Adams had calculated from the slight changes in the orbit of Uranus. The astronomer paid little attention to this letter from an unknown scientist.

Two months later a French scientist, U. J. J. Leverrier, made a similar calculation. Subsequently, he requested astronomers at the Berlin Observatory to look for the new planet in the region of the sky that he designated. They did so and discovered the new planet! Later, it was found that Adams' computations were also correct. Had attention been paid to his letter, the planet would have been discovered at an earlier date by English astronomers.

This remarkable feat of science would be regarded by many people as absolute proof of the correctness of Newton's Laws. In fact, scientists of the nineteenth century did regard it in this way. If anyone wanted to point to an absolute truth or an exact scientific law, Newton's work was generally taken as the outstanding example.

But a young man came along in 1905 and dared to doubt the perfection of Newton's work. This man was Albert Einstein, who proposed the Theory of Relativity to correct certain slight differences between the predictions of Newton's Laws and the behavior of very rapidly moving objects. Out of his work came results as startling as those of Newton. Today we have atomic energy because of the doubts which Einstein cast upon Newton's Laws.

This does not mean that Newton was all wrong. It simply means that Newton's Laws work quite well for ordinary stars, planets, and falling objects on earth, as long as they don't travel too fast. When they do, we must apply the corrections worked out by Einstein.

Are Einstein's theories perfect? Probably not. Some scientist may come along at a future date and find an error in Einstein's work. Out of such an event could come startling new discoveries.

8. GRAVITY IN SPACE

WHEN space flight becomes a reality, we will have lots of fun with gravity—or, we should say, without gravity. Out in space, with our rocket moving along at a steady speed, or in an orbiting space satellite, it will be very easy to glide across the ship. The slightest push downward against the floor would cause one to move slowly "up" to the ceiling. We put quotation marks around the word "up" because there really would be no such thing as up or down in a space ship.

Our bodies would feel most peculiar without any gravity to pull our insides down. We still are not quite sure what effect this would have on the minds of the men who might have to live with this sensation all the time.

Just think of the fun of throwing a chair to a friend at the other side of the ship. You need not throw it rapidly. Aim it carefully and give it a slight shove. Inertia takes over and the chair coasts straight across to your friend, who can catch it just as easily as you threw it.

When we arrive at the moon and begin to walk around, it will be a most delightful experience. With gravity at one-sixth of normal, a 150-pound man will weigh only 25 pounds. If a man can jump a height of three feet on earth, he can jump six times as high, or 18 feet, on the moon. If he takes a two-foot step while walking, his step on the moon will be 12 feet. If he takes a five-foot stride while running, his stride on the moon will be 30 feet! If a small house is in his way, he can simply jump over it.

BASEBALL ON THE MOON

Imagine a baseball game on the moon. If we tried to play it on a regulation field, everything would go wrong. The pitcher would throw the ball at its normal speed, because that is determined by the strength of the throw and not by gravity. But his first pitch would probably soar right over the catcher's head. After all, our pitching experience took place on earth and we learned to throw the ball at a point well above the batter's head to compensate for the amount that it falls below the straight-line path.

After some practice sessions, the pitcher learns to throw the ball across the plate for a strike. Now the batter is fooled. He expects the ball to drop as it approaches him—as it does on earth. But it only drops one-sixth as much. The confused batter would swing far below the ball. He, too, will need a number of practice sessions.

Let us suppose that pitcher and batter are now adjusted to the moon's low gravity. The batter hits the ball and starts out for first base. At the very first step, our batter is in trouble. He flies three or four feet off the ground and lands 20 or 30 feet away. In the meantime, he is flailing his arms and legs in an attempt to get his balance. The members of the team will need a substantial amount of practice before they can run properly.

Well, now everybody has adjusted to the new kind of gravity. The pitcher pitches and the batter swings. Crack! The ball starts to sail off into center field. But look at it go! It doesn't travel much faster than on earth. It's just that it seems to refuse to come down to earth—or, we should say, moon. It arches very slowly, gradually coming down about one-third of a mile from home plate. It bounces 50 or 60 feet up and finally comes to a stop a half-mile from the plate. The poor fielders have long since lost sight of the ball. They are leaping about from rock to rock, looking for it. Meanwhile, the batter has reached first in three giant leaps. He has trouble rounding first base, but there is plenty of time while the ball is sailing way out beyond the field.

After everybody who has hit the ball has gotten his home run, time is called for a consultation. The game is called off until a new ball is obtained. What kind of ball should be ordered from back home on earth? A heavier ball will not be good because when the bat hits such a ball it is likely to splinter and the batter's hands could be injured. It would be better to get a "dead ball," with little or no bounce, so made that it has about one-sixth as much bounce as an ordinary ball. It will then not travel as far when hit.

Whether this would solve the problem or not, we

really can't say. There may be other complications in fielding, running, and throwing that would only appear if an actual game were played.

GRAVITY AND THE AIR WE BREATHE

There is one thing we forgot in our imaginary baseball game. There is no air on the moon! Our players would therefore have to wear special suits. Such suits would have to contain the necessary amount of air at the right pressure to enable our players to be comfortable. An accidental puncture against a rock would have serious consequences, with life-giving air rushing out into the zero pressure (vacuum) almost instantaneously. On second thought, let's call off the game altogether. It will be difficult enough just to exist on the moon.

Why does the moon have no air? Scientists think that this is because of its low gravity. You have noticed that when gas escapes from the kitchen range it spreads throughout the kitchen and even into other rooms. The particles of the gas are in rapid motion. In fact they are moving at speeds of about one mile a second.

The moon's gravity is so low that the speeds of particles of gases, including air, are sufficient to permit them actually to fly off into space. A long time ago, the moon probably had air of some kind which has since escaped.

The earth's gravity on its surface is six times as strong as that of the moon. Therefore the chance of escape of air particles from the earth is greatly reduced, and a good part of our original air is still with us.

But some of our air has probably escaped. For example, hydrogen gas may have once existed in our atmosphere. It is a very light gas, and its particles move faster than those of gases in the air. Thus the hydrogen may have risen to the top of the atmosphere in the past, and its particles gradually shot off into space. At least, that is what some scientists think may have happened.

There is some kind of atmosphere on the planet Mars, but it is very thin compared to ours. This is easily explained by the fact that Mars is smaller than the earth—but not as small as the moon. Its gravity is therefore less than that of the earth but greater than that of the moon. So Mars has lost more air than the earth, but has not yet reached the condition of complete absence of air that exists on the moon.

GRAVITY ON OTHER PLANETS

As we go from planet to planet in a space ship, we will encounter all sorts of peculiar gravity conditions. The force of gravity on the surface of Mars is less than half of what it is on the earth's surface. Walking on Mars would therefore be great sport. We could jump more than twice as high and twice as far.

But on the planet Jupiter it would be a very different story. That planet is much larger than the earth. Gravity on its surface is more than double that on the earth's surface. Our bodies would feel like lead weights all the time. It might prove to be impossible to exist for long under these circumstances. New ailments might appear and life might be drastically shortened.

GRAVITY ZERO

We are so accustomed to Mother Earth that we rarely give a thought to the particular conditions of life on our planet. So many things would change if we wandered off into space. For example, consider such a seemingly simple matter as drinking a glass of water on a space ship where gravity is zero. You hold the glass under the faucet and turn the handle. Nothing comes out! Since there is no gravity to pull the water down, it stays in the tank. Some kind of pressure system will be needed in the tank to make the water move.

Let's say that you have solved this problem. You turn the handle and the water comes out. It hits the bottom of the glass and bounces upward. Without gravity to hold the water down, it splashes up and outward, keeps moving because of inertia, hits the ceiling, bounces off, hits the floor, bounces off, hits the walls, and so on.

Now let's assume that you arrange some kind of a cover to keep the water from spilling out of the glass. You get ready to drink, remove the cover, and bring the glass to your lips.

Whoops! The water keeps going because of inertia and flies right into your face. You put the glass "down," to wipe your face. The water bounces up as the glass hits the table, and promptly wanders off to the wall.

Fig. 33. Drinking a glass of water could be quite a problem on a space ship free of gravity.

This is getting to be quite a problem. You fill a glass of water and carefully set it on the table while you think of a way to get it to your lips. While you are engaged in your thoughts, the water is busy climbing up and over the sides of the glass, going across the table, down the table legs, onto the floor, up the walls, and perhaps even into the next room. Why did this happen?

Normally, water stays at the bottom of a glass because it is pulled down by gravity. If you look closely at the surface of water in a glass, you will see that where it touches the side of the glass it rises a bit. This occurs because of a slight force of attraction of the glass for the water, as shown by the fact that water sticks to glass and wets it. But without gravity this slight attraction of the glass for the water would pull it up and over the top and down the sides onto the table. Then the water would run onto the metal or wood of the table, down to the floor, and up the walls.

So you would have trouble drinking a glass of water in a space ship. You might have to go back to your infant days and drink it from a bottle with a nipple!

9. EARTH SATELLITE ORBIT

WE have already seen how Newton's explanation of the orbit of the moon helped set the pattern for computing the orbit of artificial satellites. In fact, the problem of figuring out the orbit of any moon around the earth (or around any other planet) is practically the same as figuring out the orbit of any planet around the sun. All of these motions have one thing in common: a smaller object revolves out in space around a larger one. With a few mathematical adjustments to take care of the different weights and distances between the objects, the resulting orbits can be quite easily calculated.

The difficult part comes when great accuracy is sought. We must then take into account the effects of gravity forces exerted by distant planets and moons. Each object pulls every other off course slightly. The computations then become quite complicated and tedious. Today automatic computers have taken a very considerable load off the shoulders of space-flight planners and astronomers by performing these complicated calculations quickly and with precision.

THE MOON'S ORBIT

Judging from our previous discussion of the paths

followed by falling objects, one might suppose that the path followed by the moon around the earth would have the same general shape—that of a parabola. After all, the moon is falling toward the earth because of gravity's pull, just as a parachutist is pulled downward. Both have inertia due to forward speed. Shouldn't their paths be somewhat similar? There is one important difference in the moon's motion that alters its path. The parachutist is near the surface of the earth and does not move very far. The downward pull of gravity is therefore practically always in the same direction.

But this is not the case for the distant moon. At A in Fig. 34 we see the moon's inertia carrying it to-

Fig. 34. Gravity force and inertia combine to make the moon follow an orbit around the earth.

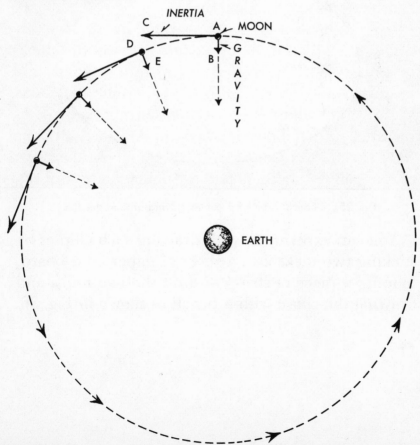

ward C while the earth's gravity pulls it toward B. These motions combine to bring the moon to D. Now note that the direction of the earth's gravity (DE) has shifted as compared with AB. Newton was able to prove that as a result of the changing direction of the pull of the earth's gravity, the path of the moon would not form a parabola but rather a closed oval-shaped orbit. The shape of this oval is called an *ellipse*.

Fig. 35 shows a typical elliptical orbit shape for a comet moving around the sun. The orbits of all the planets and moons are also ellipses, but much more nearly circular than those of comets.

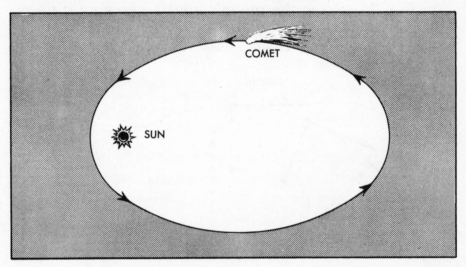

Fig. 35. Elliptical orbit of a comet moving around the sun.

You can experiment with drawing such ellipses by sticking two tacks into a sheet of paper on a board, looping a piece of string around the two nails, and drawing the curve with a pencil as shown in Fig. 36.

The locations of the two tacks used in making such a drawing of an ellipse are called foci (pronounced fosī). In the case of planetary orbits the sun is always found at one *focus* of the ellipse. In the case of an earth satellite orbit the center of the earth would always be located at one focus of the elliptical orbit.

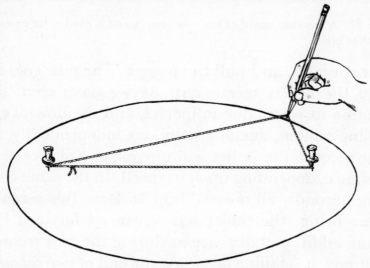

Fig. 36. How to draw an ellipse.

As a result of Newton's work scientists are today able to calculate the exact speed an earth satellite must reach and the direction in which it must go in order to go round and round the earth. Would you like to figure out the necessary speed yourself? Let's do it.

FIVE MILES A SECOND

First, imagine that you are shooting a powerful gun. Get up on the roof of a tall building, place the rifle against your shoulder, set the barrel perfectly

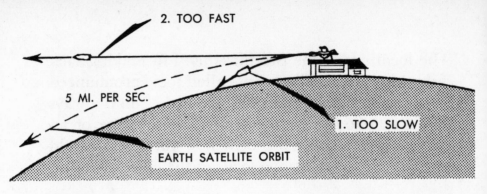

Fig. 37. A minimum speed of five miles per second is needed for an earth satellite orbit.

horizontally, and pull the trigger. The gun goes off and the bullet speeds out. As we have seen, the motion forward, due to inertia, and the downward falling motion, due to gravity, act independently. In one second, the bullet will move forward a certain distance, depending upon its speed. In the same time (one second), all objects drop 16 feet. Two seconds after firing, the bullet has advanced forward the same additional distance as during the first second. But now it is falling faster. At the end of two seconds it will have fallen 64 feet. Soon thereafter the bullet hits the ground (path No. 1 in Fig. 37).

Notice that, according to this reasoning, you should not aim a gun straight at the target in order to hit it. You should point the gun upward a bit to make allowances for the amount of drop of the bullet. Thus, if it takes one second for the bullet to reach the target, you must allow for a 16-foot drop and therefore aim at a point 16 feet above your target. Keep in mind that this is the theoretical figure which does not take air resistance into account.

Now let's suppose that you have a special gun,

with a bullet so fast that it travels a hundred thousand miles a second. In this case, the amount of fall of the bullet is so slight that it takes an almost straight path out into space, and escapes from the earth (path No. 2 in Fig. 37).

Now somewhere between the speeds in path No. 1 and path No. 2 there should be a speed that is just right so that the bullet falls an amount exactly equal to the amount of curvature of the earth. Then the bullet would be at the same height above the earth after one second as it was at the start. Now it is in an orbit. It will continue that way thereafter—except for the interference of air friction. Let's forget about air friction for a moment and consider it later.

We can restate the problem as follows. At what speed must a bullet travel so that when it is fired horizontally it moves forward and falls just the right amount to parallel the earth's surface and follow its curvature?

Suppose that we get out some surveying instruments and make a few measurements. We set up a surveying telescope on a very large level field at A in Fig. 38 and point it horizontally. The line of sight (AB) then follows the path of our extremely fast bullet.

Now we set up a tall stick near the telescope and mark a zero on it at the same level as the telescope. We measure 16 feet above this zero mark and cut off the rest of the stick above 16 feet. An assistant is then told to walk away from us, carrying the stick in a vertical position. We watch him in our telescope.

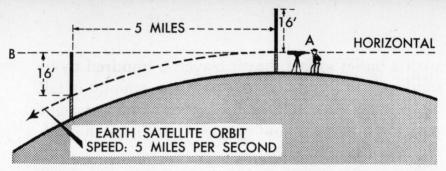

Fig. 38. A simplified way of calculating the speed needed by an earth satellite.

Soon his feet disappear around the curve of the earth. Then we see his head disappear below the horizon. Now only the stick shows. At a certain distance we see the top of the stick right on the crossed lines in our surveying telescope. We radio to our assistant to go no farther. The distance to his position is measured. We find it to be five miles. So we now know that the earth's surface curves away from a horizontal line to the extent of 16 feet at a distance of five miles.

Now let's get a rifle that has a bullet speed of five miles a second. We shoot the gun. The bullet moves forward five miles and falls 16 feet. Has it hit the ground? No, it is at the zero mark on our stick five miles away. It is at exactly the same height at which it started, and is now traveling in a direction parallel to the ground.

Inertia makes it go forward another five miles and fall 16 feet during the next second. Once again, it is back at the starting height. It is now in an earth satellite orbit. It will continue in a circular path around the earth forever—unless air friction stops it.

Don't get the idea that the bullet actually moves irregularly straight out and then down. At any particular moment it is moving forward and downward at the same time. The path therefore continuously curves and follows the earth's surface.

Scientists don't calculate the speed required for an orbiting earth satellite in the clumsy way we have described. They have much easier methods. A few minutes of mental work with Newton's Laws provides the answers to a very high degree of accuracy. A student of physics in college can apply his knowledge to make the necessary calculations. And he need not be an expert in the subject to do this.

Do you recognize the figure of five miles a second? You read about it in the newspapers as the speed of our earth satellites. It is the minimum speed that any object must reach in order to maintain a circular orbit around the earth and thus become an earth satellite.

What would happen if the speed were greater than five miles a second? Instead of paralleling the surface of the earth, the satellite would slowly rise above its original level as it circled the earth. Newton showed that it would follow an elliptical orbit, larger than the circular orbit. It would reach its highest point and lowest speed at a point exactly opposite that at which it started (B in Fig. 39). Then it would start to fall closer to the earth, speeding up as it approached, until it came back to the starting point once again moving at its starting speed and in the original direction. This process would be repeated over and over.

Let's turn our attention for a moment to the

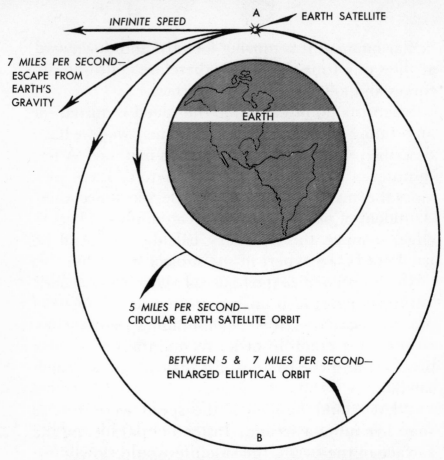

Fig. 39. The orbit of a space satellite depends upon its speed.

problem of air friction. If air gets in the way of our earth satellite to slow it down, it will spoil all our calculations.

First, the reduction in speed will cause the satellite to curve more sharply downward, and eventually it will hit the earth. Secondly, a speed of five miles a second—equal to 18,000 miles an hour—is so great that the air friction would cause enough heat to melt or even ignite the metal, and the satellite would rapidly burn up.

We can solve these problems only by starting our satellite at an altitude where there is almost no air at all. Thus earth satellites must be shot up to heights above 150 miles to get away from the atmosphere.

PLANNING AN ORBIT

Now, suppose that you are the one in charge of planning the launching of a space satellite. What is your plan?

First, get the rocket straight up, away from the earth's atmosphere. The higher you get it, the better, but it must rise at least 150 miles or so. Now turn the rocket so that it travels horizontally to the earth's surface. Then let it speed up until all the fuel is gone. If at the moment the fuel burns out the satellite is traveling more than the critical speed of five miles a second, all is well. The satellite will orbit around the earth. You have no worries if the speed is higher. The satellite will simply travel in an enlarged ellipse (Fig. 39).

You may have noticed in the newspapers that an earth satellite makes a series of parallel paths across the continents as it revolves about the earth. Why does this happen?

First, at a speed of 18,000 miles an hour, the satellite completes a trip around the 25,000-mile circumference of the earth in about an hour and a half. Actually the distance is more than 25,000 miles, because the satellite travels in an orbit larger than the earth.

Since the satellite is completely free of contact with the earth, it is no longer affected by the earth's spinning. The orbit remains in approximately the same position out in space with respect to the earth. When the satellite makes a complete turn around the earth, it comes back to almost the same position in space with respect to the earth. In the meantime, about an hour and a half have gone by. In that time, the earth has turned a bit, and the satellite passes over the earth at a point west of its previous path. Thus the combination of a fixed orbit and a rotating earth guarantees that the satellite will pass over many regions on earth during its existence.

10. CAUSING MOTION

HOW do you walk or run?

A silly question. You simply pick up your foot and . . . well, it's not as easy to explain as it seems.

Let's start with the runner in Fig. 40. We see that he has a special frame behind his feet. As soon as the gun goes off for the start of the race, he will kick back as hard as he can against the frame and take off like a streak. But if he kicks back against the frame, why does he go forward? Newton explained this with his Third Law of Motion: *To every action there is an equal and opposite reaction.*

We have seen this law at work in many of the situations discussed earlier in the book. For example, the truck colliding with a store (Fig. 8) exerted an action that pushed the store forward. On the other hand the store exerted a reaction on the truck that pushed it back. Thus both were damaged. In Fig. 10 the action of the water pushed the car upward. At the same time the reaction of the car on the water pushed the water downward, slowed it down, and made it spray sideward and downward. The earth's gravity pulls the moon downward and makes it follow an orbit. But the moon's gravity pulls the earth upward and causes the tides.

The runner pushing against the frame leaps forward because his backward action causes an equal and opposite reaction by the frame. The reaction of the frame pushes forward and makes him leap ahead.

Suppose that the runner tries the same thing on ice without any frame. The low friction of his feet against the ice would cause them to move backward and slide. There would be little action against the ice and therefore little reaction to push him forward. Thus he would not be able to run on the ice.

On regular ground there is enough friction to enable the runner to act against the ground and push backward. The ground then reacts oppositely and sends the runner forward. If the runner is on sand, the sand gives way. The runner then cannot

Fig. 40. This runner uses a supporting frame behind his feet in order to apply more backward action against the ground and thereby get more forward reaction from the ground. *(Wide World Photo)*

Fig. 41. To run or walk forward we push backward against the ground. The ground's reaction sends us forward. *(Wide World Photo)*

act as strongly against the sand and the reaction that sends him forward is then also less. Therefore his speed on sand is greatly reduced.

ACTION AND REACTION IN BASEBALL

The batter and the catcher in Fig. 41 have just started off on their respective tasks. The catcher has just missed the fourth ball and is starting after it. He pushes backward against the ground. Reaction of the ground then sends him forward.

The batter does the same thing, except that he heads for first base. He also pushes backward against the ground in order to get the ground's forward reaction that will send him on his way. As one foot pushes backward, the other foot is brought forward ready to take over the pushing job a moment later.

In Fig. 42 we see the player in the center running backward to catch a pop fly. To run backward he pushes his feet forward. This forward action causes a backward reaction from the ground which sends him backward.

The player at the right is coming up from behind to catch the ball. He slows himself down to get into proper position. How does he do it? He needs a backward force to slow down. This means that he needs a backward reaction from the ground. He gets this backward reaction by pushing in a forward direction against the ground. So he leans back, digs in, and pushes forward as he moves. The ground reacts by pushing him backward.

All of these actions against the ground require a great deal of friction to avoid slipping. Therefore baseball players wear shoes with special cleats. In-

Fig. 42. To run backward or slow down we push forward against the ground. (Wide World Photo)

creased friction then enables them to dig in and grip the ground to permit the actions and reactions to take place.

ACTION AND REACTION IN EVERYDAY LIFE

Analyze the motions that you make when rowing. The purpose of the oar and the oarlock on the boat is to provide a way of pushing backward against the water. The equal and opposite reaction of the water against the oar pushes it forward. And the boat is then pushed forward by the oar through its attachment at the oarlock.

Reaction also causes the motion of an automobile. The engine is connected to the back wheels in such a way that the bottom of the wheel pushes backward against the ground. You can see this backward push on a muddy road. When the wheels slip, mud is thrown backward. But on a hard road, the backward action of the wheels causes an opposite reaction by the road that sends the car forward.

In Fig. 43 we see a man flushing snow from a street with a powerful stream of water from a hose. Notice how he braces his body. The powerful action of the forward-moving water causes an equally powerful backward reaction that can knock him off his feet. So he sets his body forward to counteract the backward reaction and prevent the hose from moving.

Let's use reaction to invent a new kind of boat. Station a hose on a boat, pointing backward. Then pump water from the front of the boat and push it rapidly out the back. The action of the backward-moving water should then cause an equal forward reaction to make the boat move forward.

Actually we have invented nothing new. There are boats that work in a similar way. However, it is found to be less wasteful of fuel to eliminate the pump and to act against the water with a propeller that shoots water backward. The opposite reaction of the water against the propeller sends the boat forward.

Fig. 43. The action of the water shooting out of the hose produces a backward reaction against the man holding the hose. (*Standard Oil Co. of N.J.*)

Fig. 44. The propellers push air backward. The jets shoot gases backward. The forward reaction of the air to both makes the airplane move. *(Fairchild Aircraft)*

An airplane propeller works in exactly the same way. If you stand behind an airplane when it is on the ground with the propellers whirling, you feel a powerful backward breeze. This backward action of the propeller on the air causes an opposite reaction by the air that makes the airplane move forward.

The airplane in Fig. 44 makes use of special jets

Fig. 45. The upward lift needed for this "flying platform" is obtained from the downward push of a propeller against the air. *(Hiller Helicopters)*

Fig. 46. Action and reaction explain why these runners move their arms in a direction opposite to that of their legs. *(Wide World Photo)*

to assist its propellers during takeoff. This is done to get the airplane off the ground quickly on a short field or when it carries a heavy load. The jet simply shoots gases rapidly out the back. The forward reaction to the motion of the gases sends the airplane forward. A rocket engine works in a similar way.

Helicopters obtain upward lifting force by pushing air downward. The flying platform shown in Fig. 45 is a special form of helicopter with the propeller built into the base.

EFFECTS OF ACTION AND REACTION

Action and reaction show up in many interesting ways when things are in motion. As an example, notice the positions of the arms and legs of the runners in Fig. 46. Whenever the left leg is forward the left arm is backward, and vice versa. If you were to try

91

running with your hands tied to your sides, it would be rather uncomfortable and your speed would be low. If you tried running so that each arm goes forward at the same time that the corresponding leg goes forward, you would find it even more difficult to run. Your body would twist violently back and forth.

Why does this happen? The action of your leg in moving forward is always accompanied by an equal backward reaction on the rest of your body. If the left leg moves forward, then the left side of your body is pushed backward. At the same time your right leg is moving backward. The right side of your body reacts by being pushed forward. Your body therefore twists as the legs move.

However, you compensate for this twist by making your arms move in a direction opposite to that of your legs. By causing an opposite twist, the reaction to the motion of your arms cancels out the reaction effect produced by your legs and you can run with little or no twisting of the body.

The lowly fly is thought to have a similar arrangement for counteracting reaction effects. The arrow in Fig. 47 points to a small knob-shaped organ under the wing. It is thought to be a vestige of the fly's second wing. A similar knob-shaped organ is found on the other side of the fly.

High-speed photographs reveal that the two tiny wing remnants always move in a direction opposite to that of the main pair of wings. When the main wings go up, the knob-shaped wing stubs go down,

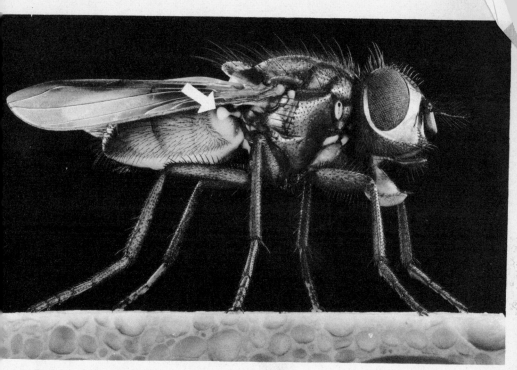

Fig. 47. A knob-shaped remnant of a wing (shown by the arrow) on the housefly vibrates in a direction opposite to that of the main wing while in flight, thus helping to counteract reaction effects. (*American Museum of Natural History*)

and vice versa. Some scientists think that the purpose of this motion is similar to the opposite motion of the arms and legs when people walk or run. Reaction effects are reduced and flight performance is improved.

A helicopter has a similar problem. The rotation of the propeller at the top causes an equal, but opposite, rotation on the body of the helicopter that tends to make it spin around in midair. Flight under such conditions would be difficult if not impossible. To counteract this rotation some helicopters are equipped

93

TAIL
ROTOR

Fig. 48. This helicopter must have a tail rotor to counteract the reaction caused by the spin of the main rotor. (*Standard Oil Co. of N.J.*)

with two propellers, spinning in opposite directions. Other helicopters, of the type shown in Fig. 48, have a small sideward propeller at the tail to make the ship tend to rotate in the opposite direction and thus keep it on course.

The propeller of an airplane with a single engine causes a similar rotational reaction, but to a smaller extent. The reaction shows up as a tendency of the airplane to dip its wing. This tendency is counteracted by constructing the airplane with a slight twist of the wings and tail.

11. LIFTING FORCES

LOOK closely at the water skier in Fig. 49. Notice that he is not using skis, but is riding on his bare feet. How can he stay up on the water?

He needs an upward lift to keep him up. He can only get an upward lift by pushing down against something, in this case the water. So he tilts his feet at an angle, as shown in Fig. 50. They strike the water as he is pulled along, and push the water down-

Fig. 49. This water skier uses his bare feet instead of skis. He makes up for the small area of his feet by going at high speed. (*Wide World Photo*)

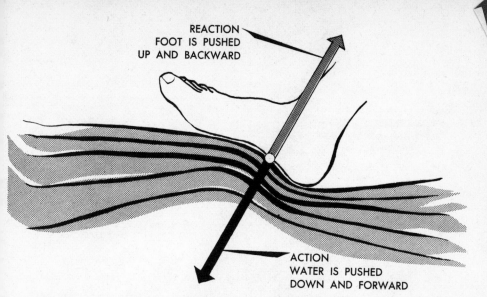

REACTION
FOOT IS PUSHED
UP AND BACKWARD

ACTION
WATER IS PUSHED
DOWN AND FORWARD

Fig. 50. The water skier obtains lift by pushing downward against the water. The water's reaction pushes him upward.

ward, causing it to move out of the way. The water reacts oppositely to force the skier upward.

His action in pushing the water out of the way as he moves forward also causes a backward reaction on him which tends to make him slow down. But in Fig. 49 we see that he is being pulled forward by the rope attached to the boat. The pull of the rope counteracts the reaction of the water that tends to slow him down.

The flying water skier and soaring boat in Fig. 51 get upward lift in a similar way. The water skier has just gone up a ramp (not shown in the photo). As he hit the ramp with his skis, he caused a downward reaction against the ramp. The ramp reacted by pushing him upward. If he causes an extra action by kicking downward with his legs, the ramp gives him an extra upward reaction that makes him jump higher.

Fig. 51. The flying water skier obtains lift by pushing down against a ramp (not shown). The flying boat obtains lift as its whirling rotor pushes downward against air. *(International News Photo)*

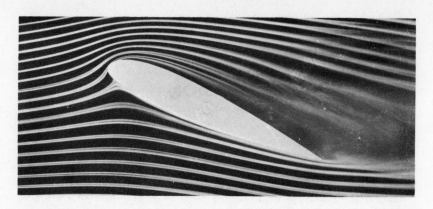

Fig. 52. Smoke streamers moving past an airplane wing reveal how lift is obtained by pushing downward against the air. Reaction by the air lifts the wing. *(National Advisory Committee for Aeronautics)*

The flying boat uses the whirling propeller above it to get lift in a similar way. The blade of the propeller is arranged to hit the air at an angle, just as the water skier tilts his skis (or feet) at an angle (as shown in Fig. 50). The downward push against the air causes the upward lift which keeps the flying boat aloft.

The wings of airplanes work in exactly the same way to get enough lift to make the airplanes fly. Notice the great resemblance between the action of air against the airplane wing in Fig. 52 and that of the water in Fig. 50.

The larger the wing, the greater the downward push against the air and the greater the upward lift on the airplane at a given speed. However, a small wing can get the same lift if the airplane goes fast enough, just as the water skier of Fig. 49 can get enough lift without skis by reaching a high enough speed.

12. ROCKET PROPULSION

YOU may have wondered why space ships use rocket engines rather than jet engines or some other kind of engine.

The ordinary kind of engine used to propel cars, buses, trucks, ships, diesel trains, and airplanes obtains its energy by burning a fuel. But the fuel will not burn unless oxygen is supplied. Therefore all of these engines have some arrangement for taking in air, which contains oxygen.

But where shall we get oxygen out in space? We can't! There is no oxygen there. If our space ship uses an engine which burns fuel, it must carry along all the necessary oxygen. This extra weight makes space flight more difficult than it otherwise would be.

ACTION AND REACTION IN SPACE

Now let us consider the method of propulsion. We have seen that in ordinary motions such as walking or rowing, and even in propeller-driven planes, the vehicle pushes backward against something to get the necessary forward reaction. We push against the ground, or against water, or against air.

But a space ship has nothing out in space against

which to push. So we see that another obstacle to space flight is that the ship must carry along its own material against which it is to push. This material will have to be hurled out the back of the ship. The reaction to this action will send the space ship forward.

However, the space ship is heavier than the material shooting out the back at any moment. How then can we obtain high speed? If we push the material out the back faster, the action is greater. Then the reaction is greater and the space ship speeds up more rapidly.

So we see that the trick in space flight is to achieve the greatest possible speed of the material shooting out the back. The low weight of the exploding gases will be compensated for by high speed. Rocket fuels are therefore selected for the high speed which the gases reach as they rush out the back.

There may come a time when ordinary fuels will no longer be used for space rockets. The speeds of atomic bullets and of electronic particles can be much higher than the speeds of burning gas particles. Future space ships may eliminate ordinary fuels and oxygen for propulsion and substitute electrical or atomic engines.

Let's imagine a trip to the planet Mars. We need a speed of at least seven miles a second to escape from the earth. Let us say that we select a cruising speed of ten miles a second. This amounts to 36,000 miles an hour. We take off from earth. The reaction to the gases hurling downward makes us move upward. We pick up speed. Suppose that every second we gain ten miles an hour in speed. Our speed at the start is then 10 mph., 20 mph., 30 mph., and so on every second thereafter.

After 100 seconds, we are going 1,000 mph. After 1,000 seconds, we are going 10,000 mph. We would reach our 36,000-mph. speed after 3,600 seconds, which happens to be exactly one hour after the start.

Then we shut off the motor. Inertia and the lack of friction are now our friends. Even though the earth is tugging at us, trying to pull us back, our speed is so great that we are soon far out in space with the earth's gravity becoming weaker and weaker as we recede from it. An occasional blast from the rocket engine suffices to maintain our speed. Inertia does the main job in getting us to Mars, without any major assistance from the rocket engine. The purpose of the rocket engine is to get us out of the earth's gravitational effect and to give us sufficient speed to coast to our destination.

The space ship now carries us toward Mars at an almost steady ten miles a second. In one hour we will have covered 36,000 miles. At the end of a 24-hour day we will be almost a million miles from earth. If Mars happens to be fifty million miles away we will arrive in its vicinity in a bit less than two months. That's not too bad for about one hour's use of fuel.

How do we land? A slowing-down action will be needed as we approach Mars. The space ship is turned around; the rockets are turned on and shoot backward. The reaction now slows the ship. Finally, we have almost stopped. We let the ship fall downward, and apply the fuel to the rocket motor in just the right amount so that its force balances the weight of the ship. We let the ship move gently downward to land.

Perhaps some kind of wing might be used to permit the ship to glide part of the way in and thus save precious fuel.

How would we steer the ship or turn it around out in space? Many methods are possible. Several small rockets around the circumference of the front of the ship would do the trick. A small blast away from the ship and to the left would send the nose of the ship to the right. A blast of a small rocket on the other side would send the ship to the left. By properly adjusting the strengths of the blasts from a number of rockets, the nose could be pointed in any desired direction.

A REACTION PROBLEM IN SPACE

Now just to see whether you have mastered the principles of space flight, let us pose a little problem. Your rocket has sprung a leak due to bombardment by a meteor particle the size of a grain of sand. You go outside the ship in your space suit, carrying along some tools and material to fix the leak. As you finish the repair job, you gleefully pat the side of the ship. To your surprise, the slight push causes the backward reaction to propel you away from the ship. For a moment you are interested in this effect. Then suddenly, in horror, you realize that you have moved beyond the reach of the safety bars around the ship —and you forgot to take the normal precaution of tying your rope to a bar.

Now inertia is your enemy. You keep moving away from the ship at a slow but steady speed. The distance keeps increasing. Your instinct is to walk back. But you can't! There is nothing to push against. If you don't do something fast, you may be lost out in space forever.

Suddenly you remember Newton. You take a wrench and throw it with all your might in a direc-

Fig. 53. You could move around in space by throwing objects in a direction opposite to that in which you want to go.

tion away from the ship. It sails off into space. But its backward reaction sends you toward the space ship. However, since you threw "from the shoulder," the reaction is applied to the top part of your body and you start to rotate head over heels, but at least approaching the ship all the time. As you near the ship, rotating all the while, you see that you will miss it by a few feet. With a carefully calculated throw another tool is hurled out into space and its reaction alters your path sufficiently for you to reach the ship. You heave a sigh of relief.

Just imagine where you would be if you hadn't learned about Newton's Laws.

13. CURVING MOTION

CENTRIFUGAL AND CENTRIPETAL FORCE

THE skier in Fig. 54 is engaged in a slalom contest in which he must swoop down a mountainside, swerving in and out between a series of posts. This means that he must change his normal straight-line motion into a swerving motion.

How can he swerve to his right? He will need a force pushing him to his right. He gets this force by pushing sideward against the snow in a direction opposite to the way he wants to swerve. The snow reacts to his action and pushes him in the direction he wants to go. Notice how he leans toward the inside of the turn in order to push sideward against the snow.

Fig. 54. We swerve on a turn by pushing sideward against the outside of the turn. Reaction sends us inward to make the turn. (*Wide World Photo*)

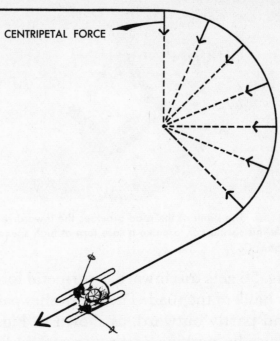

CENTRIPETAL FORCE

Fig. 55. Centripetal force is needed to enable a skier to make a turn.

If you think of his curving motion as being circular in form, the skier's outward force may be thought of as pointing away from the center of the circle. This kind of outward push by the skier against the ground is called the *centrifugal force*. The inward force which the snow exerts against him and which makes him move in a circular arc is called the *centripetal force,* as shown in Fig. 55.

BANKING ON A TURN

Any vehicle moving in a curve must create an inward or centripetal force to push it sideward and overcome its tendency to move in a straight line because of inertia. The car racing around the track in

Fig. 56. The bank of the road provides the inward reaction needed to enable this racing car to make a safe turn at high speed. *(Firestone Tire and Rubber Co.)*

Fig. 56 gets this inward centripetal force from the tilt or bank of the road. The car pushes partly downward and partly outward, as shown in Fig. 57. The road reacts by pushing partly upward and partly inward. The upward push holds up the car. The inward push makes the car go into a curve.

Careful examination of Fig. 56 reveals that the track slopes more steeply on the outside part of the curve. As a car goes faster, it needs more inward force to round a curve safely. The driver can use the steep outside part of the track to obtain the larger inward centripetal force that he needs to make a rapid turn. For slower turns the driver can use one of the inner sections of the track with less slope.

Modern roads are generally banked around turns. The engineer who designs the road sets the angle of bank at the best one for the particular amount of curve and for the speed at which he estimates the cars will travel.

If a car rounds a sharp curve that does not have any tilt, the inward centripetal force needed to make the turn can only come from friction of the tires against the road as the front wheels turn. If the tires are too smooth, if the road is wet or icy, or if the turn is made too fast, friction may not be enough to push the car sideward to make the turn. It may then skid off the road in a straight line, due to inertia. If at any time during such a skid the car turns sideward to the direction in which it is moving, friction tends to slow down the bottom of the car while inertia tends to make the top of the car keep going. The top may thus move faster than the bottom and cause the car to turn over.

Fig. 57. How a banked road provides inward force when a car makes a turn.

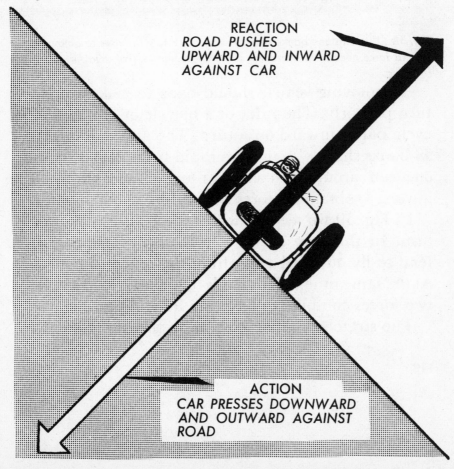

REACTION
ROAD PUSHES
UPWARD AND INWARD
AGAINST CAR

ACTION
CAR PRESSES DOWNWARD
AND OUTWARD AGAINST
ROAD

Fig. 58. This airplane banks sharply on a quick turn in order to obtain the inward force needed to overcome straight-line inertia. *(Fairchild Aircraft)*

Any moving vehicle should bank to make a rapid turn properly. The rider of a bicycle or of a motorcycle banks inward on a turn. The airplane in Fig. 58 banks sharply to make a rapid turn. Watch someone run around a corner. You will see him lean inward to obtain the force he needs to make the turn.

In Fig. 59 we see a different method of making a turn. In this case the people in the whirling seats tend to fly outward away from the center (Fig. 60). At the same time weight tends to make them fall. The two forces combine to form the force AB in Fig. 60.

The stretched cable lines up in the direction AC

in order to balance the combination of outward centrifugal force plus weight. The inward pull of the cable creates the centripetal force that is needed for the circular motion. It also creates the upward force that holds up the weight of the person in the seat.

People in a turning vehicle experience centrifugal force as a tendency to be thrown outward. If the door of a car is not properly closed, it may fly open on a rapid turn, and its occupants may actually fall out. This centrifugal force on a turn is really inertia operating to keep everything in the car moving straight ahead.

But when the seat is angled properly, as occurs on a banked road, centrifugal force and weight combine to push the car's occupants perpendicularly against

Fig. 59. The cables of this whirling ride take a sharp banking angle because inertia tends to make the riders continue in straight-line motion. *(Standard Oil Co. of N.J.)*

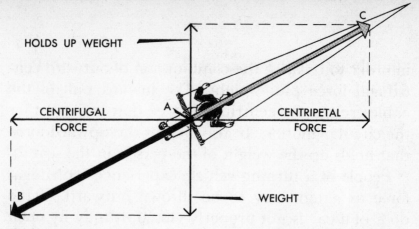

HOLDS UP WEIGHT

CENTRIFUGAL
FORCE

A

CENTRIPETAL
FORCE

B

WEIGHT

C

Fig. 60. As the speed of the turn increases, the angle of bank increases to provide the larger inward force needed to make the turn.

the seat without any tendency to slide outward. The proper position of the occupants in relation to the seat is shown in Figures 57 and 60.

If the rate of rotation is rapidly increased, centrifugal force may soon exceed a person's weight. A person in a properly banked vehicle will then feel his "weight" to be much more than normal. Men have been subjected to such large "weights" in special rotating machines. Small organisms have been subjected to forces 10,000 times that of gravity by whirling them in special "centrifuges." Practical use is made of such machines to force heavy particles to settle out of liquid mixtures. If a glass of water contains a very fine clay that might take weeks to settle to the bottom, the use of a centrifuge will cause the clay to settle in a matter of minutes. Such machines are of great value to chemists and doctors.

CENTRIFUGAL FORCE AND THE EARTH

In Chapter 7 it was mentioned that people weigh

slightly less at the equator than at the North Pole. Centrifugal force is responsible for this reduction in weight.

As the earth rotates, centrifugal force tends to throw all objects outward, just as mud is hurled away from the hub of a spinning wheel. You may think of the earth as a giant spinning wheel with the North and South Poles as the hub and the equator as the outside of the wheel. The greatest centrifugal force is found at the outside of the wheel—at the equator. The material in the earth tends to fly outward from the "hub." As a result the earth bulges outward at the equator.

Objects at the equator weigh less for two reasons. First, they are farther from the center of the earth because of the bulge, and gravity is therefore slightly less. Second, the tendency to be hurled outward by centrifugal force opposes gravity and makes all objects a bit lighter.

The planet Jupiter is much larger than the earth, yet spins more rapidly. As a result it has a very pronounced bulge at its equator, much more than that of the earth.

Could a planet have a very rapid rate of rotation? A spin that is too rapid would cause the parts of a planet to fly off into space, thus leading to its destruction. In the laboratory we can experiment with this effect by rotating a wheel more and more rapidly until it flies apart with almost explosive force. Such experiments are conducted to test the strength of materials.

Fig. 61 shows an unusual application of centrifugal force. It looks as though the gentleman in this whirligig will tend to fall on his head when he reaches the top of the ride. But if the speed of rotation is rapid enough, his tendency to be thrown outward from the center may become great enough to balance his weight. It is possible for him to make a complete turn around and be pushed upward against the frame at the top of the ride, without any tendency to fall.

You can try a simple experiment to show this effect. Take a small pail with a handle. Fill the pail halfway to the top with water and whirl it around and around over your head in a vertical circle. The water will stay in the pail even when it is upside down at the top of the circle. (It might be a good idea to wear a bathing suit just in case the water spills out!) Centrifugal force on the water is greater than its weight and keeps it in the pail at the top of its path.

Now slow down the rotation. At a certain speed the water will spill out. Centrifugal force is less than the weight of the water at this reduced speed, and gravity pulls the water down.

The orbit of a planet or earth satellite may be explained by centrifugal and centripetal force. Think of the satellite whirling in a circle around the earth as tending to fly outward because of centrifugal force. What makes it veer from a straight line and travel in a circle? Centripetal force is needed.

Fig. 61. Centrifugal force hurls this man outward at high speed and keeps his feet against the outside of the frame even when he is upside down. (Wide World Photo)

Gravity is that force. The earth satellite will stay in a circular orbit when the centrifugal force (outward-flying tendency) due to its speed is just balanced by centripetal force (inward pull of gravity). The satellite then acts just like a weight whirled around your head on the end of a string, except that the invisible pull of gravity takes the place of the string.

Centrifugal force also explains the weightless feeling that will be found in an earth satellite. An orbit is achieved when the speed of the satellite is such that centrifugal force balances gravity. A person who is pulled toward earth with a force of 150 pounds (his weight) is then thrown outward with an equal centrifugal force. Since these forces are equal and opposite on every part of his body, they cancel each other and the person feels completely weightless.

A SUBSTITUTE FOR GRAVITY

Centrifugal force has certain interesting similarities to gravity force, although it is different in other ways. For example, imagine a giant space ship which is set spinning around its long center line. All the people and objects in it would tend to be thrown outward, away from the center (Fig. 62). Centrifugal force would act as a substitute for gravity. But the people would stand "up" in the ship with their feet "down" on the inside of the wall and with their heads pointing toward the center.

"Gravity" in this ship would be different from ours. If one climbed a ladder toward the center of

Fig. 62. Centrifugal force could be used as a substitute for gravity in a large space ship. But a fellow right in the center would feel rather mixed up. Why would this not be practical in a space ship six feet in diameter?

the ship, the centrifugal force would become less and less. Finally, at the center it would disappear. A person who got right in the center would have a most peculiar feeling of being torn apart, with centrifugal force pulling his head "up" and pulling his legs "down" at the same time.

However, you can see that a large spinning space ship would offer a practical way to obtain an artificial kind of gravity. It would be possible for people to live in such a space ship under more normal conditions.

You may have seen drawings in the newspapers of large doughnut-shaped earth satellites. This doughnut shape is proposed because it would provide a constant imitation of gravity if it were set spinning like a wheel.

Of course, everybody may be fooled. It may turn out that being free of gravity is such a pleasurable experience that people would prefer it. But that remains to be seen when the first man ventures out into space.

14. CHANGING SPEEDS

WE have seen how Newton's First Law, that of *inertia,* explains the motions of objects when no forces are acting on them, or when the forces are balanced. Later we discussed Newton's Third Law, which deals with *action and reaction* and the way in which motion can be produced. The Second Law of Motion has been left for last because it is a bit more difficult than the others, and involves some mathematics. However, we have selected some of the simpler aspects of this law to show its general idea.

Newton's Second Law deals with *acceleration* and *momentum*. In other words, it deals with the things that occur when objects are speeded up or are stopped.

SPEEDING UP

Look at the pitcher throwing a ball in Fig. 63. Notice that his arm is far back and his left leg is off the ground. Newton's Second Law will help us to understand why he throws the ball in this manner.

Suppose that we apply a large force to an object that is at rest. The force causes it to move. As long as the force keeps acting, and is not balanced by other forces such as friction, the object will accelerate (speed up). When the force is balanced by friction or other forces, the object no longer speeds up. It then coasts along at steady speed under the influence of inertia.

Obviously, if you push harder the object will speed up more rapidly and reach a higher speed. Our pitcher must have strong muscles in order to push the ball as hard as he can.

But he has another way to increase the speed of the ball. This method involves know-how rather than brute strength. He (or his coach) can make use of Newton's Second Law.

What will happen if you allow the force more *time* in which to act? It seems reasonable to suppose that if the force produces a certain speed in one second, it would produce even more speed in two seconds, and still more in three seconds.

Thus, to speed up the ball, a pitcher pushes it as hard as he can, and tries to push it *for as long a time as possible*. He can push the ball for a longer time if he pushes it for a longer distance. So the pitcher gets his arm as far back as he can, starts pushing the ball, brings his arm around, shifts to his other leg, continues to push, and doesn't let go until the arm is as far forward as he can get it. The combination of a lot of force applied for a comparatively long interval of time enables him to throw a fast ball.

The same thing applies to the batter. He puts his bat way back and starts pushing it faster and faster without letup around a wide circle. The coach calls this the "follow-through." A coach in tennis, in golf,

Fig. 63. A good pitcher throws a fast ball by pushing the ball for a longer time. (Life *Photo by Francis Miller, copyright 1955 by Time, Inc.*)

and in any other sport involving throwing or hitting an object will always give the same advice. By following-through in a wide powerful swing you allow more time for the force to act and therefore achieve a much higher speed.

Notice the javelin thrower in Fig. 64. In which direction will he hurl the javelin? Don't answer too

Fig. 64. This javelin thrower achieves higher speed and a longer throw by making a complete about-face and hurling his javelin off to the left. The resultant longer pushing time gives him greater speed. (Wide World Photo)

quickly. If you try to imitate his position, you will find that he is about to make a complete about-face. The starting line is at the left of the picture, behind him! He is about to whirl his javelin around and throw it off to the left. His purpose in doing this is to make a longer throw by utilizing Newton's Second Law. The turnabout gives him more time for pushing, and therefore enables him to achieve a higher speed and make a longer throw.

In the hammer throw a large heavy ball on the end of a wire is whirled around and around, faster and faster, until the thrower releases it to soar off into space. The purpose in whirling the heavy ball around several times is to give the force more time to act, and thus to reach a higher speed.

In Fig. 65 we see how this law applies when a football is kicked. The high-speed x-ray photo shows

Fig. 65. The air in a football gives way and then bounces back. As a result the ball is in contact with the foot for a longer time and reaches a higher speed. (*International News Photo*)

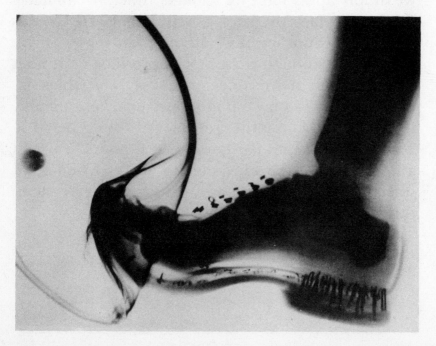

how the foot penetrates deeply into the ball. The ball is filled with air, a fact which makes a big difference in the way the football moves. If the ball were filled with cement, its inertia would tend to stop the toe, to the kicker's great pain. But the air is compressible. This means that it can be squeezed to a great extent. Once squeezed it is under pressure and tends to return to its original shape. It starts to do so even as the force of the foot is pushing it. But it takes a certain time before it springs back to shape. All this while it is being pushed by the foot. As a result the ball is pushed for a much longer time than if the air were not inside the ball. This longer pushing time gives the ball more speed and it goes farther.

A HIGH-SPEED SPACE SHIP

Newton's Second Law of Motion can be put to use in rocket propulsion. A rocket need not have an enormous push in order to achieve a high speed. If we simply apply force for a longer time, we can make up for the fact that it is small. If a given force is enough to cause speeding up, no matter how slight, then, given enough time, it can produce enormous speeds. Thus, if we accelerate at a rate which increases our speed by 100 miles per hour in a minute, in one hour (60 minutes) our speed would be 60 × 100, or 6,000 miles per hour. In ten hours, it would amount to 60,000 miles per hour. Yet when a car starts it can accelerate at a rate much faster than this!

The difference is that the car can't keep on speeding up much beyond 100 miles an hour because of the rapid increase in friction at high speeds. But with friction absent in outer space, there is no such limit on the gain of speed of a space ship.

There is a limit, but of a different kind. No space ship could go faster than 186,000 miles a second, the speed of light. The reason for this limit takes us beyond Newton to Albert Einstein and his Theory of Relativity. All we shall say in this book is that Einstein has corrected Newton's Laws of Motion so that they fit the observed facts when objects begin to go at extremely high speeds. Objects that move at speeds of thousands of miles a second seem to gain in mass (become heavier and heavier). As they approach the speed of light, mass (heaviness) becomes so great that it becomes harder and harder to make them go any faster with a given push. As a result, the top limit is 186,000 miles a second—at least as far as we know today.

SLOWING DOWN

On June 25, 1957, the newspapers reported that a man had jumped or had fallen from the fifteenth-floor window of a New York skyscraper. He hit a skylight on an adjacent two-story building, broke through it and struck a metal air-conditioning duct, and finally landed on the floor of an office in the building, after falling 160 feet. The amazing thing about this event is that the man lived.

Newton's Second Law helps explain why this man did not die instantaneously. We have seen that if a force is applied for a longer time, it causes an object to reach a higher speed. This force must push in the same direction as the moving object. But suppose that the force pushes in a direction *opposite* to the motion? In that case the force will cause slowing down instead of speeding up. And the longer the force acts, the greater is its slowing-down effect. For example, if you step on the brakes of a speeding car for five seconds you will slow it down much more than if you step on the brakes for only one second.

In the case of a falling object that hits the ground, the amount of slowing down is settled in advance. We know that it will lose *all* of its speed and finally come to rest on the ground. The question remains as to the method of slowing down. Shall we permit the object to hit the hard ground and have its speed stopped in a very short time? The short stopping time will require a large stopping force. Or shall we allow more time for the force to act, and thereby reduce the amount of force needed? Newton put it this way:

$$F \times T = M \times V$$
Force × Time = Mass × Velocity
Impulse = Momentum

Let's put this formula into words. If you apply a force (F) to an object for a certain amount of time

(T), you will cause an object with mass (M) to change its velocity by an amount equal to (V). The above formula enables a scientist to calculate the amount of change in velocity produced by a force in a given time.

Examine the left side of this formula. The *impulse,* or cause of the change in motion, is measured by force (F) multiplied by the time (T). We can get the same amount of impulse by using one pound of force for ten seconds, or ten pounds of force for one second, or two pounds of force for five seconds. All of these combinations multiply to equal ten. The impulses in all three cases are therefore the same.

Looking at the right side of the formula, we see the *momentum,* $M \times V$. Although mass and weight are not exactly the same, for our purposes we may think of them as the same. The momentum of a one-pound object moving ten feet a second is the same as that of a five-pound object moving two feet a second, or a ten-pound object moving one foot a second. All of these combinations multiply to ten, and therefore represent the same amount of momentum. The three objects will be equally hard to stop.

Notice in Fig. 66 that a puny man in the lower right-hand corner of the picture is actually moving the tremendous mass of the loaded barge. This is possible for two reasons. First, friction in water is small at very low speeds. Thus his small force can overcome friction. Then he can make up for the small force he applies by allowing more time for it to act. If he patiently pulls the barge for a minute or so, he can move it appreciably.

On the other hand, the barge is so heavy that even at low speed it can have enough momentum to cause great damage. In other words, $M \times V$ is large because M is large.

You may have seen the way a ferryboat is stopped as it pushes against the groaning planks of its slip. These planks give way gradually and allow more time for the stopping force to overcome the enormous momentum of the heavy ferryboat.

In Fig. 67 we see how firemen make use of Newton's Second Law. The man jumping from the building will have a very considerable momentum when

Fig. 66. The man moving these massive barges makes up for the small force he applies by pulling for a longer time. *(United States Steel Corp.)*

Fig. 67. The momentum of the jumper can be safely overcome by increasing the time during which the stopping force acts. *(Ewing Galloway)*

Fig. 68. This acrobat makes use of Newton's Second Law to jump safely from a height. *(International News Photo)*

he reaches the ground because of his weight and high speed. And there won't be much time for stopping, because the concrete does not give way. Therefore the stopping will have to take place with a tremendous amount of force. The concrete can take this force without damage, but the man can't.

So we put Newton's Second Law to work. The time for stopping is increased by holding up a net to catch the falling man. The men hold the net high above their heads. They let it move downward as the jumper hits it. This will allow more stopping time and thus reduce the force needed. A large force is still needed, as is shown by the fact that about ten men are used for this task. But at least the force is reduced to a point where the jumper can be stopped without injury. The softness and flexibility of the material of the net also help by smoothing out the effect of the force on the jumper.

The man jumping from a window in Fig. 68 makes use of the same idea to slow himself down to a safe landing speed. By catching the wire with the handle of an umbrella, he obtains a gradual slowing-down force and so reduces the force needed to stop himself.

An even more remarkable jumping stunt is performed by the man in Fig. 69. He somersaults through the air from a 40-foot height. He then strikes the table with his hands and lands on his feet on the large cushion on the floor. In slowing himself down he makes use of four methods. Let's see if you can figure them out. Then compare your answer with the one on page 145.

Fig. 69. This man makes a living by somersaulting from a height of 40 feet. How does he make use of Newton's Second Law? (*Wide World Photo*)

Figs. 67, 68, and 69 enable us to understand how it was possible for a man to fall fifteen stories and still be alive. From the news report we learned that he crashed through a skylight and then through a metal air-conditioning duct before hitting the floor. These structures are not massive and rigid like a concrete floor. They give way and break before a large force. But each reacted, before being broken, to slow down the falling man. As a result the time for stopping his fall was greatly increased and the force required was reduced enough to prevent instant death.

Fig. 70 shows an interesting application of Newton's Second Law. We see a *raw* egg, dropped from the top of an eleven-story building, bouncing off a special rubber mat on the sidewalk! The rubber mat obtains its ability to absorb the shock by giving way and thus allowing more time for stopping force to be applied.

Your car rides smoothly because of the many parts that give way gradually when forces hit the car. When the car hits a hole in the road, the shock is absorbed gradually by the air in the tires, by the springs under the body, by the special shock absorbers, by the springs and cushioning of the seats, and by the flesh on your body. All of these work together to increase the time for the slowing-down force and thereby reduce the amount of force needed. As a result, you get a smooth ride.

SPACE FLIGHT

How do these facts affect space flight? We have

Fig. 70. This raw egg bounces safely off the rubber mat after dropping eleven floors! (United States Rubber Co.)

already seen how the reaction to the action of gases shooting out the back of a space ship can make it move at high speed. Yet at any given moment the weight of the gases coming out the back is very small in comparison with the weight of the ship. How can these light gases give an enormous velocity to a heavy space ship?

Let us picture the situation as similar to that of a bullet fired from a gun. The explosive force of the burning gases inside the gun presses forward on the bullet and equally backward on the gun barrel. Thus the action of the gases shoots the small bullet forward, and at the same time the reaction kicks the gun backward. Since the gases act for an equal time on both bullet and gun, and the amount of action and reaction is the same, one might expect the gun to kick back as rapidly as the bullet. However, the bullet has a small mass (m) while the gun has a large mass (M). The gun therefore has more inertia and is harder to move. The same force acting for the same time does not produce as much speed in the gun as in the bullet. We get a moderate kick against the shoulder from the gun barrel, rather than the effect of the speed of a bullet. The effect of the force of the backward blow is absorbed as the body moves with it, allowing more time for the stopping force to act.

Now suppose that the gun is 1,000 times as heavy as the bullet and that the bullet shoots out with a speed of 1,000 miles per hour. Since the gun is 1,000 times as hard to move, it moves back at 1/1,000 the

135

speed of the bullet—at a speed of only one mile per hour.

Now let us imagine that the gun is a space ship far away from the earth's gravity, and the bullet is our propelling mechanism. We shoot one bullet. The gun moves in the opposite direction with a speed of one mile per hour. We shoot another bullet. The gun speeds up to two miles an hour. We shoot a third, a fourth, a fifth, and then many bullets. Each bullet adds one mile an hour to the speed of the gun. It is clear that we can reach a high speed in this way. But we will soon run out of bullets.

To make a space flight it is clear that we will have to take many bullets along (or fuel for our exploding gaseous bullets). But we can also make better use of our bullets by giving them higher speed. If we get an improved bullet that shoots out twice as fast, it will then react on the gun (or space ship) to produce twice the former speed. Thus, to improve the efficiency of our rocket engines it is necessary to give the exploding gases the greatest possible speed. Then a much smaller amount of gas will produce a much larger effect in propelling the ship.

In a sense, this is the major design problem of space-ship engines. New fuels are constantly being sought which will shoot the gases out with higher and higher speeds. Experiments are being made in an attempt to find atomic and electrical methods of achieving higher and higher particle speeds. If these speeds can be raised to ten times what they are now, trips to the moon and planets will be relatively easy. If the speeds of the propelling particles can be increased to 100 times what they are now, trips to distant stars may become practical.

Put in your bid now for the first trip to Mars. At the rate at which scientists are improving rocket engines, it looks very much as though the ancient dreams of mankind for flight through space will soon be brought to reality.

15. JUST FOR PRACTICE

NOW that you have learned about force and motion, let's see if you can put your knowledge to work.

Fig. 71 shows the paths of two balls that have been pushed from a height onto two metal plates. Both show parabolic paths. But one bounces and shows a

Fig. 71. Can you explain the motion of these two balls, using the facts you have learned about force and motion? *(Westinghouse)*

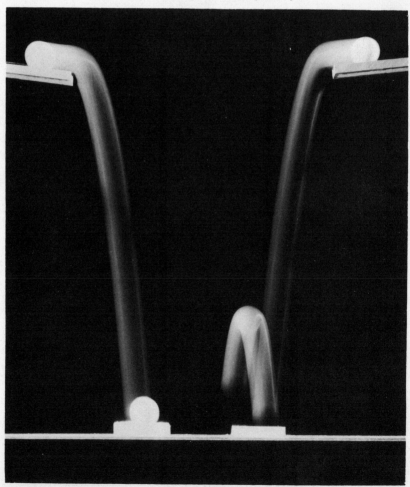

second parabolic path. The other doesn't. Explain the action of each, then compare your answer with the one on page 145.

Incidentally, this photo shows an interesting application of atomic energy. The ball on the left is made of a puttylike silicone gum. The ball on the right is made of the same material but was subjected for two seconds to bombardment with electrical par-

Fig. 72. Why is the deer's face uninjured by flying glass? *(International News Photo)*

ticles at 2,000,000 volts. This vulcanized it and changed it into a rubbery bouncing material.

Our second practice problem involves an unusual photo of a deer leaping through a glass window (Fig. 72). The deer somehow got into the building and then leaped out the window to escape.

Notice that the deer's eyes are open and its face and body seem to be unscratched at the moment this picture was taken. We can't vouch for what happened later, but it is possible, if the deer jumped rapidly enough, that it went through the window without serious injury from flying glass. Can you explain, using the laws of motion, how this could happen? Compare your answer with the one on page 146.

And now for our final problem. Notice the position of the ski jumper in Fig. 73. Why does he take this position?

If his body starts to turn in midair, how can he use his arms to maintain his position?

How is the ski run built so as to increase the length of the jump? Turn to page 147 for the answer.

Fig. 73. How does this ski jumper make use of the laws of force and motion? (Wide World Photo)

ANSWERS
TO PROBLEMS

ANSWERS TO PROBLEMS

PAGE 21, INERTIA PROBLEM

1. Inertia of motion of the car caused the force which broke the hydrant.

2. Inertia of rest of the hydrant helped stop the car, damaged it, and brought it to rest right over the broken hydrant.

3. Inertia of motion of the gushing water, stopped by the car, exerted enough force to lift the car.

4. Inertia of the car, at rest above the water, caused the water to change its direction and spray sideward and downward after hitting the car.

PAGE 30, FRICTION PROBLEM

1. As rope slides through one's hands, friction can cause the skin to rub off, just as sandpaper rubs down wood. Gloves are therefore used to protect the hands from the effects of friction.

2. The thick, rough rope has a great deal of friction. As the rope is wound around the posts, over and under other sections of rope, friction increases very rapidly. Finally it is great enough to hold the barges together. If the barges pull apart slightly, this will cause the ropes to tighten more securely around the iron posts. This tightening force serves to increase friction still more.

3. If you place an object on a board and tilt the board by lifting one end, friction holds the object in position until a certain angle is reached. Look back at Fig. 11 to see this effect. Piles of coal act in the same way. If the coal pile is too

steep, friction is not great enough to keep the pieces from rolling down the slope. But as the coal rolls down the mound, the slope becomes less steep. Finally, at a definite angle which is the same for all the piles of coal, there is enough friction to keep the coal from rolling and the angle is thereafter maintained.

PAGE 32, GRAVITY PROBLEM

1. The water in the river is pulled down over the cliff by gravity and thus creates the falls.

2. The river flows because it is pulled to lower levels by gravity.

3. Why is the water surface flat? Any high point in the water is immediately pulled down by gravity to the level around it.

4. If you look closely, you will see a boat in the river. It floats because its weight (caused by gravity) is less than that of an equal volume of water.

5. Rocks are loosened by the water and form piles at the base of the cliff when pulled down by gravity. High mountains are eventually worn down in a similar way.

6. Buildings, posts, and smokestacks are made vertical because of the effects of gravity. A building that leans away from the vertical tends to be toppled by gravity, and must therefore have extra support. We avoid the expense of such supports by making most structures vertical.

7. Why are buildings made of strong materials like wood, brick, cement, stone, and steel? The upper parts of a building are pulled down by gravity and squeeze the lower parts. As a result the structure must be strong enough to prevent gravity from making it fall apart.

8. Why do trees tend to grow straight upward? A tree can

only survive in a forest if it grows straight up to get its share of life-giving light from the sun. The tree will grow better if the roots go straight down to the water that has been pulled down by gravity. The tree somehow senses "up" and "down" by reacting to gravity force. Thus, no matter what the position of the seed when buried in the ground, the tiny stem that forms always grows upward and the tiny root always grows downward.

9. Roads are made horizontal where possible and steep hills are avoided because of gravity.

10. The ground is relatively flat because of gravity.

11. People stand and walk in a vertical position with their feet under them to avoid being pulled down by gravity.

PAGE 46, PARACHUTIST PROBLEM

After three seconds of fall the parachutist will have advanced 90 feet from his starting point and will be 144 feet below it. Since the airplane advances forward at the same rate of speed, he will still be directly below the plane.

PAGE 49, BARREL PROBLEM

1. To avoid damage to the barrels they should hit the ground at as low a speed as possible. The falling speed of the barrels is reduced by flying the plane close to the ground. Thus the barrels fall for a short distance and hit the ground with low speed. In addition the pilot flies the plane as slowly as he can, to reduce the forward speed of the barrels. If the speed of the plane is 50 miles an hour and the barrels are simply dropped out, they will have that forward speed when they hit the ground, in addition to the speed due to falling. By shooting the barrels out the back a large part of the forward speed is canceled out, thus reducing the impact.

2. Suppose that the airplane shoots barrels out the back at one-second intervals. Consider two seconds of flight of the airplane. The barrel that left the airplane two seconds ago has been dropping all that time. In two seconds it falls 64 feet. The barrel that shot out one second later has had one second in which to fall. It has therefore dropped only 16 feet. The third barrel is just being dropped from the airplane. If you refer back to Fig. 25 you will see that these three barrels form the same kind of parabola as in that figure, except in reverse.

PAGE 131, JUMPING PROBLEM

1. The cushion on the table helps to slow the acrobat down by giving way and allowing more time for the stopping force to act.

2. The cushion on the floor does the same thing.

3. As the acrobat hits the table with his arms he allows them to bend, thus permitting more time for the stopping force to act.

4. And he does the same with his knees as he lands on his feet.

PAGE 139, BALL PROBLEM

The original motion of each ball is continued after it has been pushed off the boards at a height. Inertia, combined with gravity, produces the parabolic path in each case.

The ball on the right has been made elastic by the electron bombardment. This means that it gives way when it hits the metal plate, and quickly returns to its original shape. When it strikes the plate, the material of the ball on the right gives way gradually until the ball is completely stopped. The stopping force comes from the upward reaction of the plate to the action of the ball in hitting it. After being stopped, the ball tends to spring back to its original shape. This tendency to spring back exerts a downward force on the plate, and the plate reacts upward to push the ball up, giving it enough speed to rise from the ground, and thus bounce. The ball's original forward speed due to its inertia continues to act to make it describe a second parabola.

Notice that the bouncing ball does not return to its original height. This shows that the speed of the ball after it bounces is much less than when it hit the plate. Some of the motion has been lost.

The ball on the left does not have this property of bouncing back to shape. The material simply gives way and flattens out on the plate. If you look closely, you will see that the ball did move forward slightly after hitting the plate, because of its inertia. However, friction was great enough to make it stop in a very short time.

PAGE 140, DEER-JUMPING PROBLEM

Inertia of the deer forces the window to move outward. The window reacts by pushing back at the deer. If the glass were thick enough, it would give way only a short distance before it stopped the deer. The short stopping time would cause a large force and injure the animal. However, the glass is fragile. A fraction of a second after being hit, it breaks. At that moment it no longer exerts stopping force. The short time before it breaks is not enough to injure the deer or to stop it appreciably. Inertia of the deer now carries it past the glass, pushing the pieces out of the way.

Since the deer's face touches only the broad, flat side of the glass, it is not cut. As the pieces of glass are pushed by the deer, they tend to fly outward in straight lines. If the deer is moving rapidly enough, it may be able to pass through before the pieces have time to fall. As a result, it is possible that the deer may not suffer any injury at all.

PAGE 140, SKI-JUMPING PROBLEM

The ski jumper's body position is similar to that of the wing of an airplane in flight. As he moves forward and downward against the air, his outstretched body pushes it out of the way. Inertia of rest of the air causes it to resist his motion with an upward force that makes him slow down and soar instead of falling in a normal parabolic path. As a result he can greatly extend the distance of his jump.

He can help maintain his position in midair by rotating his arms. He has a choice of two directions of rotation and a choice of rotating either arm. Any rotation of an arm will cause a reaction on his body that will tend to make it turn in the opposite direction. If he rotates his arms correctly, it is possible for him to maintain this position all the way down.

We should also note the role of inertia and of gravity in this ski jump. To start his jump the ski jumper glides down a steep runway, utilizing gravity and the low friction of the packed snow to attain great speed. He bends his knees and his body to reduce air resistance and thus increase his speed. At the moment of takeoff he suddenly kicks downward and uses the upward reaction of the slide to leap high into the air. Also, at the takeoff end the slide is curved upward to give him an initial upward motion, thereby increasing the length of his jump.

As he lands on the slope, he can avoid injury because of the fact that he is slowed down very gradually by the low friction of the ice.

Date Due

DEC 2 0 '68			
NOV 17. 70			